Economic Battleground

Navigating the 2024 US Elections

Copyright © 2024 by RK Books

All rights reserved.

No part of this publication may be reproduced, distributed, or transmitted in any form or by any means, including photocopying, recording, or other electronic or mechanical methods, without the prior written permission of the publisher, except in the case of brief quotations embodied in critical reviews and certain other non-commercial uses permitted by copyright law.

This book is a work of fiction. Names, characters, places, and incidents are products of the author's imagination or are used fictitiously. Any resemblance to actual events, locales, or persons, living or dead, is entirely coincidental.

ISBN: 978-969-52-9281-5   E-Book

ISBN: 978-969-52-9282-2   Paper-Back

ISBN: 978-969-52-9283-9   Hard-Back

Published by |

Table of Contents

Introduction 1

Chapter 1 The Historical Context of Economic Policies in Elections 4

    The Great Depression and New Deal Policies 5

    Reaganomics: Supply-Side Economics in the 1980s 9

    The 2008 Financial Crisis and its Political Repercussions 15

Chapter 2 Key Economic Issues in the 2024 Elections 22

    Inflation and Cost of Living 22

    Income Inequality and Wage Stagnation 27

    Federal Budget and National Debt 32

Chapter 3 Candidates Economic Platforms 38

    Tax Reform Proposals 38

    Approaches to Healthcare Spending 44

    Plans for Infrastructure Investment 51

Chapter 4 The Role of the Federal Reserve 60

    Interest Rate Policies and Economic Growth 60

    The Fed's Response to Economic Crises 64

    Balancing Inflation and Unemployment 68

Chapter 5 Taxation and Fiscal Policy Debates 73

    Progressive vs. Regressive Taxation 73

    Corporate Tax Policies 78

    Government Spending Priorities 83

Chapter 6 Healthcare Economics 89

    The Cost of Universal Healthcare 89

    Impact of Healthcare Policies on Small Businesses 92

    Public vs. Private Healthcare Systems 96

Chapter 7 Job Market and Employment Policies 101
- Strategies for Reducing Unemployment 101
- The Gig Economy and Labour Rights 105
- Impact of Automation on Jobs 109

Chapter 8 Trade and Globalization 113
- US-China Trade Relations 113
- The Future of Free Trade Agreements 117
- Protecting Domestic Industries 120

Chapter 9 Economic Inequality 125
- Wealth Distribution Trends 125
- Policies to Address Poverty 131
- The Impact of Education on Economic Mobility 138

Chapter 10 Environmental Economics 145
- The Economics of Climate Change Mitigation 145
- Renewable Energy Investments 151
- Balancing Economic Growth with Environmental Protection 155

Introduction

Economic Battleground: Navigating the 2024 US Elections aims to unravel the complex interplay between economic policies and political strategies in one of the most critical elections in recent American history. The year 2024 presents a unique convergence of economic challenges and opportunities that will significantly influence the direction of the United States. As voters head to the polls, their decisions will be shaped by a multitude of factors, including historical precedents, current economic conditions, and the promises made by candidates. This book seeks to provide a comprehensive understanding of these dynamics, equipping readers with the knowledge to navigate the economic battleground of the 2024 US elections.

The historical context of economic policies in elections sets the stage for our exploration. By examining pivotal moments such as the Great Depression and the New Deal, Reaganomics in the 1980s, and the aftermath of the 2008 financial crisis, we gain insights into how economic strategies have shaped electoral outcomes and national policies. Understanding these historical precedents is crucial as they often serve as reference points for contemporary policy debates and voter expectations.

As we move into the current landscape, key economic issues in the 2024 elections come to the forefront. Inflation, income inequality, and the federal budget are just a few of the pressing concerns that voters will consider. Each of these issues has far-reaching implications for the nation's economic stability and the well-being of its citizens. This book delves into these topics, providing a detailed analysis of the economic challenges and the proposed solutions from various political perspectives.

A critical component of the electoral process is the economic platforms of the candidates. In 2024, the major candidates present diverse approaches to taxation, healthcare, and infrastructure investment. By dissecting these platforms, we can compare and contrast the different visions for America's economic future. This section highlights the potential impacts of these policies on various sectors of the economy and different demographic groups.

The role of the Federal Reserve, often an overlooked aspect of electoral discussions, is another key focus. The Fed's monetary policies, including interest rates and responses to economic crises, play a significant role in shaping the economic environment. This book examines how the Federal Reserve's actions intersect with electoral politics and influence voter perceptions and candidate strategies.

Taxation and fiscal policy debates are perennial features of US elections. The 2024 elections are no different, with contentious discussions on progressive vs. regressive taxation, corporate tax policies, and government spending priorities. By exploring these debates, we provide readers with a clear understanding of the fiscal choices facing the nation and their potential consequences.

Healthcare economics remains a crucial issue, particularly in light of recent global health challenges. This book analyses the economic implications of different healthcare policies, from the cost of universal healthcare to the impact on small businesses and the debate between public and private healthcare systems.

Employment policies and the job market are at the heart of economic discussions. Strategies for reducing unemployment, addressing the gig economy, and mitigating the impact of automation are all critical topics covered in this book. The analysis provides insights into how candidates' plans might affect the workforce and overall economic health.

Trade and globalization, economic inequality, environmental economics, and technological advancements are additional focal points. Each chapter offers an in-depth exploration of these areas, highlighting their significance in the 2024 elections and their broader economic implications.

Finally, public opinion and economic perception, as well as post-election economic strategies, round out our comprehensive examination. Voter attitudes, media influence, and social media's role are scrutinized to understand their impact on economic perceptions and electoral outcomes.

Chapter 1

The Historical Context of Economic Policies in Elections

Understanding the historical context of economic policies in elections is crucial for grasping the dynamics of the 2024 US elections. Throughout American history, economic conditions and policies have significantly influenced electoral outcomes and shaped the nation's political landscape. This chapter delves into key moments when economic strategies played pivotal roles in elections, providing a foundation for analysing contemporary issues.

We begin with the Great Depression and the New Deal, examining how Franklin D. Roosevelt's policies transformed the American economy and political expectations. Moving to the 1980s, we explore Reaganomics and its impact on economic thought and electoral politics, highlighting the shift towards supply-side economics. The 2008 financial crisis and its aftermath offer insights into how economic turmoil can reshape political priorities and voter behaviour.

By tracing these historical developments, this chapter sets the stage for understanding the economic battleground of 2024. It illuminates the enduring connection between economic policies and electoral success, offering lessons that resonate in today's political debates. This historical perspective is essential for anyone looking to navigate the complexities of the current election and anticipate its potential outcomes.

The Great Depression and New Deal Policies

The Great Depression, a catastrophic economic downturn that began in 1929 and lasted throughout the 1930s, stands as one of the most significant periods in American history. It profoundly affected the nation's economic policies and political landscape. The crisis reached its nadir with the stock market crash of October 1929, leading to widespread unemployment, bank failures, and a dramatic decline in both industrial output and consumer spending. The economic turmoil of this era set the stage for a series of transformative policies under President Franklin D. Roosevelt, collectively known as the New Deal.

The Great Depression: Causes and Early Impacts

The Great Depression's origins are multifaceted, involving both domestic and international factors. In the United States, the 1920s saw a period of economic boom known as the "Roaring Twenties," characterized by significant technological advancements and industrial growth. However, this prosperity was built on shaky foundations, including over-speculation in the stock market, excessive borrowing, and uneven wealth distribution.

When the stock market crashed on October 29, 1929, also known as Black Tuesday, the immediate effect was a massive loss of wealth. The crash triggered a chain reaction: banks, many of which had invested heavily in the stock market, faced insolvency; businesses could not secure loans and began to fail; and consumer confidence plummeted, leading to reduced spending and further economic contraction. By 1933, unemployment had soared to 25%, and industrial production had halved from its 1929 levels.

The Election of Franklin D. Roosevelt

The Hoover administration's response to the Great Depression was widely seen as inadequate. Herbert Hoover, who served as President from 1929 to 1933, believed in limited government intervention and trusted that the economy would self-correct. His policies, such as the Smoot-Hawley Tariff which raised import duties, were counterproductive and exacerbated the economic downturn.

In the 1932 presidential election, Franklin D. Roosevelt, then Governor of New York, emerged as the Democratic candidate promising a "New Deal for the American people." His campaign focused on proactive government intervention to revive the economy, in stark contrast to Hoover's approach. Roosevelt's message resonated with the electorate, leading to a landslide victory.

The First New Deal (1933-1934)

Upon taking office in March 1933, Roosevelt immediately set to work implementing his New Deal policies, aimed at providing relief, recovery, and reform. The First New Deal, spanning from 1933 to 1934, focused on emergency measures to address the immediate suffering caused by the Depression.

- **Emergency Banking Relief Act:** One of Roosevelt's first actions was to stabilize the banking system. The Emergency Banking Relief Act of 1933 allowed the government to inspect and reopen solvent banks while providing support to those in trouble. This move restored public confidence, and deposits soon flowed back into banks.

- **Federal Emergency Relief Administration (FERA):** Established to provide direct relief to the unemployed, FERA funded state and local governments to create jobs and support the needy. This program laid the groundwork for later, more extensive public works initiatives.

- **Civilian Conservation Corps (CCC) and Public Works Administration (PWA):** These programs aimed at reducing unemployment through large-scale public works projects. The

CCC focused on environmental conservation projects, employing young men in reforestation, soil erosion control, and park development. The PWA funded major infrastructure projects like highways, dams, and public buildings, stimulating both job creation and economic activity.

- **Agricultural Adjustment Act (AAA):** This act sought to boost agricultural prices by reducing surpluses. The government paid farmers to leave a portion of their land fallow, thereby decreasing production and increasing crop prices. Although it faced criticism and legal challenges, the AAA helped stabilize the agricultural sector.

- **Tennessee Valley Authority (TVA):** The TVA was a bold experiment in regional planning and development. It aimed to modernize the Tennessee Valley, a region severely affected by poverty and lack of infrastructure, through the construction of dams, electrification projects, and initiatives to improve agriculture and industry.

The Second New Deal (1935-1938)

Building on the initial successes, Roosevelt introduced the Second New Deal, which focused on more extensive social and economic reforms. This phase sought to provide long-term security and stability through systemic changes.

- **Social Security Act of 1935:** One of the most enduring legacies of the New Deal, the Social Security Act established a system of old-age benefits, unemployment insurance, and aid to families with dependent children. This act marked a significant shift towards a welfare state, providing a safety net for the elderly, unemployed, and vulnerable populations.

- **Works Progress Administration (WPA):** The WPA was an ambitious public works program that employed millions of

Americans in a wide variety of projects, from constructing roads and buildings to creating art and literature. It was instrumental in reducing unemployment and improving the nation's infrastructure.

- **National Labour Relations Act (Wagner Act):** This act strengthened the rights of workers to organize and bargain collectively. It established the National Labour Relations Board (NLRB) to oversee labour disputes and protect workers' rights, leading to a significant increase in union membership and worker protections.

- **Rural Electrification Administration (REA):** The REA aimed to bring electricity to rural areas, which were lagging behind urban centers in infrastructure development. By funding the construction of power lines and promoting cooperative ventures, the REA drastically improved the quality of life and economic opportunities in rural America.

Impacts and Legacy

The New Deal had a profound and lasting impact on American society and governance. Economically, it helped to stabilize the banking system, reduce unemployment, and stimulate industrial and agricultural recovery. While the Depression did not fully end until World War II's economic boom, the New Deal mitigated some of its worst effects and laid the groundwork for future growth.

Politically, the New Deal reshaped the American political landscape. It expanded the role of the federal government in the economy and introduced the concept of a social safety net. Roosevelt's policies fostered a new coalition of voters, including urban workers, African Americans, and rural farmers, which transformed the Democratic Party into the dominant force in American politics for decades.

The New Deal also faced criticism and resistance. Some conservatives argued that it expanded government power too much and threatened individual liberties, while some liberals felt it did not go far enough in addressing economic inequalities. Despite these criticisms, many New Deal programs became permanent fixtures of American life, and the era is often cited as a model for governmental intervention in times of economic crisis.

The Great Depression and the New Deal policies represent a pivotal chapter in American history, illustrating the profound impact of economic crises on policy and governance. Roosevelt's bold initiatives not only aimed to revive the economy but also to reform it fundamentally, ensuring greater security and equity for American citizens. As we navigate the economic challenges of today, the lessons from this era remain highly relevant, demonstrating the potential of innovative policy responses to address complex economic problems.

Reaganomics: Supply-Side Economics in the 1980s

Reaganomics refers to the economic policies promoted by U.S. President Ronald Reagan during the 1980s. These policies were rooted in supply-side economics, a theory that argues economic growth can be most effectively fostered by lowering taxes and decreasing regulation. Proponents of supply-side economics believe that when businesses and individuals are less burdened by taxes and regulatory constraints, they invest and spend more, thus driving economic expansion. Reagan's economic agenda marked a significant shift from the Keynesian policies that had dominated U.S. economic policy since the New Deal era.

The Context: Economic Challenges of the 1970s

Before delving into the specifics of Reaganomics, it is important to understand the economic environment of the 1970s, which set the stage for Reagan's policies. The decade was characterized by "stagflation "a combination of stagnation (slow economic growth and high unemployment) and inflation (rising prices). Traditional Keynesian approaches, which advocated for increased government spending to stimulate demand, seemed ineffective against stagflation.

Several factors contributed to this economic malaise:

1. **Oil Crises:** The 1973 oil embargo and the 1979 Iranian Revolution led to sharp increases in oil prices, exacerbating inflation and slowing economic growth.

2. **High Government Spending:** The costs associated with the Vietnam War and the Great Society programs contributed to significant federal budget deficits.

3. **Regulatory Environment:** Many industries were heavily regulated, leading to inefficiencies and limited innovation.

   This economic stagnation led to a growing belief that a new approach was needed one that focused on boosting the supply side of the economy.

Key Components of Reaganomics

Reaganomics can be summarized through four main pillars: tax cuts, deregulation, reducing government spending, and monetary policy.

1. **Tax Cuts**

A cornerstone of Reaganomics was the belief that reducing taxes would spur economic growth. The Economic Recovery Tax Act of 1981 (ERTA), often referred to as the Kemp-Roth Tax Cut, was the most significant piece of legislation in this regard. It reduced the top marginal tax rate from 70% to 50% and cut the tax rate for the lowest income earners from 14% to 11%. Additionally, it aimed to encourage savings and investments by offering various incentives.

The logic behind these tax cuts was based on the Laffer Curve, which posited that lower tax rates could lead to increased tax revenues by boosting economic activity. The idea was that people would have more money to spend and invest, leading to job creation and higher overall economic growth.

2. Deregulation

Another key aspect of Reaganomics was deregulation. The administration sought to reduce the regulatory burden on businesses, believing that excessive regulation stifled innovation and growth. This policy extended across various sectors:

- **Transportation:** Deregulation of the airline and trucking industries aimed to increase competition and lower prices.

- **Banking and Finance:** Reforms such as the Garn-St. Germain Depository Institutions Act of 1982 allowed for greater flexibility in the financial industry, encouraging savings and investment.

- **Environmental and Occupational Regulations:** The Reagan administration rolled back many regulations that were perceived as overly burdensome to businesses.

3. Reducing Government Spending

While Reaganomics is often associated with reducing government intervention in the economy, in practice, cutting government spending proved challenging. Although the administration aimed to decrease spending on domestic programs, defence spending increased significantly during Reagan's tenure, driven by his desire to confront the Soviet Union in the Cold War.

Efforts to cut spending included reducing funding for social programs such as welfare, food stamps, and federal education programs. However, the overall impact on government spending was mixed due to the substantial increase in defence expenditures.

4. Monetary Policy

Reaganomics also included a focus on controlling inflation through monetary policy. While the Federal Reserve operates independently of the executive branch, Reagan supported the Fed's efforts under Chairman Paul Volcker to combat inflation through tight monetary policy. This approach involved raising interest rates to reduce the money supply, which successfully brought down inflation from double-digit levels in the early 1980s to around 4% by the end of Reagan's presidency.

Economic Outcomes

The implementation of Reaganomics led to a period of significant economic change, marked by both successes and criticisms.

1. Economic Growth and Job Creation

The U.S. economy experienced a period of robust growth during the 1980s. After a recession in the early years of Reagan's presidency, the economy rebounded, with GDP growth averaging around 3.5% annually from 1983 to 1989. The unemployment rate, which had peaked at 10.8% in 1982, fell to 5.3% by the end of Reagan's second term.

2. Inflation and Interest Rates

The combination of supply-side tax cuts and tight monetary policy helped bring down inflation. High interest rates initially contributed to a recession, but as inflation decreased, the Federal Reserve gradually lowered interest rates, which further stimulated economic growth.

3. Budget Deficits and National Debt

One of the most controversial aspects of Reaganomics was its impact on the federal budget deficit and national debt. Despite efforts to cut domestic spending, the substantial tax cuts and increased defence spending led to significant budget deficits. The national debt tripled from around $900 billion in 1980 to $2.7 billion in 1989.

4. Income Inequality

Critics of Reaganomics argue that the benefits of economic growth were unevenly distributed. Income inequality increased during the 1980s, with the wealthiest Americans seeing significant gains while middle- and lower-income families experienced more modest improvements. The reduction in social program funding also disproportionately affected the poor and vulnerable populations.

Legacy of Reaganomics

Reaganomics left a lasting legacy on U.S. economic policy and political discourse. The emphasis on tax cuts, deregulation, and reduced government intervention in the economy influenced subsequent administrations and continues to shape economic policy debates today.

1. Shift in Economic Philosophy

Reaganomics represented a fundamental shift away from Keynesian economics towards a supply-side approach. This shift emphasized the role of private enterprise and market forces in driving economic growth, a philosophy that has remained influential in Republican economic policy.

2. Debates on Tax Policy

The tax cuts of the Reagan era sparked ongoing debates about the effectiveness of supply-side economics. Proponents argue that the policies led to significant economic growth and job creation, while critics contend that they disproportionately benefited the wealthy and increased income inequality.

3. Impact on Government Spending

Reagan's efforts to reduce the size of government and cut social programs set a precedent for future policy discussions. The tension between reducing government spending and maintaining essential services remains a key issue in American politics.

4. Deregulation

The deregulation initiatives of the 1980s had long-term impacts on various industries, particularly finance. The increased flexibility in the financial sector contributed to economic growth but also laid the groundwork for future financial crises, including the Savings and Loan crisis of the late 1980s and early 1990s, and the 2008 financial crisis.

Reaganomics marked a significant era in American economic policy, characterized by a shift towards supply-side economics. The policies implemented under President Reagan had profound effects on economic growth, inflation, government deficits, and income inequality. While the long-term benefits and drawbacks of Reaganomics continue to be debated, its influence on the economic and political landscape is undeniable. Understanding Reaganomics provides valuable insights into the evolution of U.S. economic policy and the ongoing debates that shape it.

The 2008 Financial Crisis and its Political Repercussions

The 2008 financial crisis, often referred to as the Great Recession, was a catastrophic economic downturn that had profound impacts on the global economy and political landscape. Originating in the United States, the crisis was the result of a complex interplay of financial innovations, regulatory failures, and risky lending practices. Its aftermath reshaped economic policies and political dynamics both in the U.S. and around the world.

Causes of the 2008 Financial Crisis

The seeds of the 2008 financial crisis were sown years before its onset. Several key factors contributed to the financial meltdown:

1. **Housing Bubble and Subprime Mortgages**

   During the early 2000s, the U.S. experienced a housing boom fuelled by low interest rates, easy credit, and financial innovation. Banks and mortgage lenders, eager to profit from the rising housing market, began issuing a significant number of subprime mortgages to borrowers with poor credit histories. These risky loans were often bundled into mortgage-backed securities (MBS) and sold to investors, spreading the risk throughout the financial system.

2. **Financial Innovation and Risky Practices**

   The widespread use of complex financial instruments like collateralized debt obligations (CDOs) and credit default swaps (CDS) contributed to the crisis. These instruments were designed to manage and distribute risk but instead created layers of opacity and systemic vulnerability. Rating agencies, incentivized by fees from issuers, often assigned high ratings to these risky securities, misleading investors about their true risk.

3. **Regulatory Failures**

   Regulatory oversight failed to keep pace with the rapid financial innovation. Key regulatory bodies, including the Securities and Exchange Commission (SEC) and the Federal Reserve, did not adequately monitor or address the growing risks in the housing and financial markets. The repeal of the Glass-Steagall Act in 1999, which had previously separated commercial and investment banking, also contributed to increased risk-taking by financial institutions.

4. **Global Imbalances**

   Global economic imbalances, such as the large trade deficits of the U.S. and the surpluses of exporting countries like China, played a role in the crisis. These imbalances led to massive capital inflows into the U.S., driving down interest rates and encouraging excessive borrowing and investment in housing.

The Collapse and Immediate Aftermath

The crisis reached its peak in 2008, beginning with the collapse of major financial institutions:

1. **Bear Stearns and Lehman Brothers**

   In March 2008, Bear Stearns, a major investment bank, faced insolvency due to its exposure to toxic mortgage assets. It was acquired by JPMorgan Chase with government assistance. The failure of Lehman Brothers in September 2008, however, marked the most dramatic event of the crisis. Lehman's bankruptcy triggered a panic in financial markets, leading to a severe credit freeze and a cascade of failures among financial institutions worldwide.

2. **Government Interventions**

   In response to the crisis, the U.S. government took unprecedented steps to stabilize the financial system. The Troubled Asset Relief Program (TARP), enacted in October 2008, authorized $700 billion to purchase distressed assets and inject capital into banks. The Federal Reserve also implemented aggressive monetary policies, including slashing interest rates to near zero and launching quantitative easing programs to inject liquidity into the economy.

Economic and Social Impacts

The economic and social impacts of the 2008 financial crisis were severe and widespread:

1. **Unemployment and Foreclosures**

   The crisis led to massive job losses, with the U.S. unemployment rate peaking at 10% in October 2009. Millions of Americans lost their homes due to foreclosures, as falling home prices and rising mortgage defaults created a vicious cycle.

2. **Global Recession**

   The U.S. crisis quickly spread to other countries, leading to a global recession. Trade collapsed, and many countries experienced severe economic contractions, leading to widespread hardship and political instability.

3. **Wealth Destruction**

   The crisis wiped out trillions of dollars in household wealth, particularly affecting retirement savings and home equity. The resulting loss of consumer confidence further depressed economic activity.

Political Repercussions in the United States

The political repercussions of the 2008 financial crisis were profound, reshaping the political landscape in the U.S.:

1. **Election of Barack Obama**

    The economic turmoil played a significant role in the 2008 presidential election, aiding Barack Obama's victory. Obama campaigned on a platform of change and promised to address the economic crisis with decisive action. His administration's early efforts focused on economic stimulus, financial reform, and stabilizing the housing market.

2. **Dodd-Frank Act**

    In response to the crisis, the Dodd-Frank Wall Street Reform and Consumer Protection Act was signed into law in 2010. This comprehensive financial reform aimed to reduce the likelihood of future financial crises by increasing oversight and regulation of financial institutions. Key provisions included the creation of the Consumer Financial Protection Bureau (CFPB), stricter capital requirements for banks, and the Volcker Rule, which limited speculative trading by banks.

3. **Rise of the Tea Party Movement**

    The financial crisis and subsequent government bailouts led to a backlash against perceived government overreach and fiscal irresponsibility. This backlash contributed to the rise of the Tea Party movement, a conservative faction within the Republican Party that emphasized reducing government spending, lowering taxes, and limiting the size of government. The Tea Party had a significant impact on the 2010 midterm elections, helping Republicans gain control of the House of Representatives.

4. **Polarization and Populism**

   The crisis exacerbated political polarization and fuelled populist sentiments. Many Americans felt that the government had favoured Wall Street over Main Street, leading to deep mistrust of both financial institutions and political leaders. This sentiment set the stage for the rise of anti-establishment candidates in subsequent elections, including the election of Donald Trump in 2016, who capitalized on voter anger and disillusionment with the political and economic status quo.

Global Political Repercussions

The 2008 financial crisis also had significant political repercussions globally:

1. **Eurozone Debt Crisis**

   The financial crisis exposed vulnerabilities in the Eurozone, leading to a sovereign debt crisis. Countries like Greece, Ireland, Portugal, Spain, and Italy faced severe fiscal crises, necessitating bailout packages from the European Union and the International Monetary Fund. Austerity measures imposed as part of these bailouts led to widespread social unrest and political upheaval in affected countries.

2. **Global Regulatory Reforms**

   In the aftermath of the crisis, global financial regulatory frameworks underwent significant changes. The Basel III accord introduced stricter capital and liquidity requirements for banks. The Financial Stability Board (FSB) was established to coordinate international efforts to enhance financial stability and prevent future crises.

3. **Shift in Economic Power**

   The crisis accelerated the shift in economic power towards emerging markets, particularly China. As advanced economies struggled with recovery, emerging markets demonstrated resilience and continued to grow, altering the global economic balance.

Long-Term Impacts and Lessons

The long-term impacts of the 2008 financial crisis continue to shape economic policies and political dynamics:

1. **Economic Inequality**

   The crisis highlighted and exacerbated economic inequalities. The recovery was uneven, with wealthier individuals and large corporations benefiting significantly from rising asset prices, while many middle- and lower-income families struggled with stagnant wages and job insecurity.

2. **Financial Regulation and Stability**

   The reforms implemented in response to the crisis have improved financial stability, but debates continue about their adequacy. Critics argue that some measures have been rolled back or undermined, potentially leaving the financial system vulnerable to future crises.

3. **Trust in Institutions**

   The crisis eroded public trust in financial and political institutions. Rebuilding this trust remains a critical challenge for policymakers, who must balance the need for effective regulation with fostering economic growth and innovation.

   The 2008 financial crisis was a defining event in modern economic and political history. Its causes, impacts, and repercussions have reshaped economic policies, regulatory frameworks, and political dynamics in the U.S. and globally. Understanding the crisis and its aftermath provides valuable insights into the vulnerabilities and strengths of the global financial system, the importance of effective regulation, and the ongoing challenges of economic inequality and political polarization.

Chapter 2
Key Economic Issues in the 2024 Elections

The 2024 US elections are set against a backdrop of significant economic challenges and opportunities, making economic issues a central focus for voters and candidates alike. This chapter explores the most pressing economic concerns that will shape the election discourse and influence voter decisions. Key topics include the persistent threat of inflation, which affects the cost of living and purchasing power for everyday Americans, and income inequality, a growing issue that impacts social cohesion and economic stability. Additionally, the federal budget and national debt continue to be critical concerns, with debates over fiscal responsibility and funding priorities taking center stage. Understanding these issues is crucial for navigating the complex economic landscape of the 2024 elections and evaluating the proposals and platforms of the candidates vying for office. This chapter aims to provide a comprehensive overview of these pivotal economic topics, offering insights into their implications for the future of the United States.

Inflation and Cost of Living

Inflation, the rise in the general level of prices for goods and services over time, is a crucial economic issue that significantly impacts the cost of living. As inflation increases, the purchasing power of money declines, meaning that consumers need more money to buy the same goods and services. The cost of living, which includes expenses such as housing, food, healthcare, and transportation, becomes higher as inflation rises. In the context of the 2024 US elections, understanding the causes, effects, and potential policy responses to inflation is essential for voters and policymakers alike.

Understanding Inflation

Inflation can be categorized into two main types: demand-pull inflation and cost-push inflation.

1. **Demand-Pull Inflation** occurs when the demand for goods and services exceeds supply, causing prices to rise. This can happen due to various factors, including increased consumer spending, government expenditure, or investment. When the economy grows rapidly, demand for products and services increases, leading to higher prices.

2. **Cost-Push Inflation** happens when the costs of production increase, and businesses pass these costs onto consumers in the form of higher prices. This can be caused by rising wages, increased prices for raw materials, or supply chain disruptions.

Recent Trends in Inflation

The United States has seen significant fluctuations in inflation rates over the past few decades. Most recently, the COVID-19 pandemic and its aftermath have had a profound impact on inflation. The initial economic shock of the pandemic led to a brief period of deflation, but as the economy began to recover, inflationary pressures emerged.

Several key factors have contributed to the recent surge in inflation:

1. **Supply Chain Disruptions:** The pandemic caused widespread disruptions in global supply chains, leading to shortages of goods and materials. These shortages have driven up prices for a wide range of products, from electronics to automobiles.

2. **Labor Market Tightness:** As businesses reopened, many faced challenges in hiring workers, leading to wage increases. Higher wages contribute to higher production costs; which businesses often pass on to consumers through higher prices.

3. **Increased Demand:** Government stimulus measures, including direct payments to individuals and expanded unemployment benefits, boosted consumer spending. This increased demand, particularly for goods over services, put upward pressure on prices.

4. **Energy Prices:** Rising energy costs, driven by factors such as geopolitical tensions and production constraints, have broad implications for inflation. Higher fuel prices increase transportation and production costs across the economy.

Impact on Cost of Living

The rise in inflation directly affects the cost of living, making it more expensive for individuals and families to cover their basic needs. This impact is felt across various sectors:

1. **Housing:** Housing costs, including rent and home prices, have risen sharply in recent years. Low interest rates and high demand have driven up home prices, while rent increases are squeezing tenants. Housing affordability has become a significant concern, especially in urban areas where demand far outstrips supply.

2. **Food and Groceries:** Food prices are particularly sensitive to inflation. Factors such as increased transportation costs, supply chain disruptions, and higher labor costs have led to rising prices for groceries. This trend places a heavier financial burden on households, particularly those with lower incomes who spend a larger proportion of their income on food.

3. **Healthcare:** The cost of healthcare in the United States has been rising for years, and inflation exacerbates this issue. Higher costs for medical services, prescription drugs, and health insurance premiums add to the financial strain on individuals and families.

4. **Transportation:** Higher fuel prices directly increase the cost of commuting and travel. Additionally, transportation costs affect the prices of goods that rely on shipping and logistics, further driving up the cost of living.

5. **Utilities and Services:** Inflation also affects the cost of utilities such as electricity, water, and heating. These rising costs, along with higher prices for other essential services, contribute to the overall increase in the cost of living.

Policy Responses to Inflation

Addressing inflation and its impact on the cost of living requires a comprehensive approach that includes monetary policy, fiscal policy, and regulatory measures:

1. **Monetary Policy:** The Federal Reserve (Fed) plays a critical role in managing inflation through its control of interest rates and the money supply. By raising interest rates, the Fed can cool down an overheated economy, reducing consumer and business spending, which can help bring inflation under control. However, this approach can also slow economic growth and increase unemployment, so it must be carefully managed.

2. **Fiscal Policy:** Government spending and taxation policies can influence inflation. Reducing government spending or increasing taxes can help decrease demand-pull inflation. Conversely, targeted fiscal measures, such as subsidies or tax relief for essential goods and services, can help mitigate the impact of rising prices on vulnerable populations.

3. **Supply-Side Measures:** Addressing supply chain disruptions and increasing the supply of goods and services can help alleviate cost-push inflation. This might involve investing in infrastructure, promoting domestic production, and removing regulatory barriers that hinder supply chains.

4. **Wage Policies:** Ensuring that wages keep pace with inflation can help protect the purchasing power of workers. This might involve setting higher minimum wages or encouraging wage growth through labor market policies. However, care must be taken to avoid triggering a wage-price spiral, where higher wages lead to higher prices, which in turn lead to demands for even higher wages.

Political Implications for the 2024 Elections

Inflation and the cost of living are likely to be central issues in the 2024 elections, influencing voter behavior and shaping campaign strategies. Candidates will need to address these concerns convincingly to gain voter support.

1. **Voter Concerns:** Rising prices and the cost of living are tangible issues that affect everyday life. Voters are likely to prioritize candidates who propose effective solutions to control inflation and alleviate financial pressures. This makes economic policy a critical battleground in the upcoming elections.

2. **Policy Proposals:** Candidates will need to present clear and practical plans to address inflation. This may include specific measures to control housing costs, healthcare expenses, and food prices, as well as broader economic strategies to stabilize prices and promote sustainable growth.

3. **Economic Messaging:** Effective communication about economic policy will be crucial. Candidates must explain how their policies will benefit ordinary Americans and provide relief

from rising costs. This involves not only addressing immediate concerns but also presenting a vision for long-term economic stability and prosperity.

4. **Political Accountability:** The handling of inflation and economic challenges will also impact perceptions of political accountability. Voters will scrutinize the actions taken by current leaders and their effectiveness in managing the economy. This could influence their decisions at the ballot box.

Income Inequality and Wage Stagnation

Income inequality and wage stagnation are pivotal economic issues that have far-reaching implications for the overall health of the economy and social cohesion. These issues are likely to play a significant role in the 2024 US elections as they impact millions of Americans' everyday lives. This chapter delves into the causes, consequences, and potential solutions for income inequality and wage stagnation, providing a comprehensive understanding of their significance in contemporary economic and political discourse.

Understanding Income Inequality

Income inequality refers to the uneven distribution of income across various segments of society. In the United States, income inequality has been increasing for several decades, with the gap between the wealthiest and the poorest widening significantly. Several factors contribute to this trend:

1. **Technological Advancements:** Automation and technological innovation have disproportionately benefited high-skilled workers while reducing demand for low-skilled labour. This has led to higher wages for those with specialized skills and stagnant or declining wages for others.

2. **Globalization:** The integration of global markets has led to outsourcing and offshoring of many manufacturing and service jobs. While globalization has brought overall economic growth, it has also resulted in job losses and wage suppression for certain segments of the workforce.

3. **Decline of Unions:** Union membership has declined significantly over the past few decades. Unions have traditionally played a crucial role in negotiating higher wages and better working conditions. Their decline has weakened workers' bargaining power, contributing to wage stagnation.

4. **Policy Decisions:** Tax policies and regulatory changes have often favoured capital over labour. Lower tax rates on capital gains and high-income earners, coupled with reduced social safety nets, have exacerbated income inequality.

5. **Education and Skill Disparities:** Access to quality education and training opportunities is uneven, leading to significant skill gaps. Those with higher education and specialized skills command higher wages, while those without such credentials are left behind.

Wage Stagnation

Wage stagnation refers to the lack of significant growth in real wages over time, adjusted for inflation. Despite increases in productivity and economic growth, many American workers have not seen corresponding increases in their pay checks. Several factors contribute to wage stagnation:

1. **Productivity-Wage Gap:** While productivity has increased, wages have not kept pace. The benefits of increased productivity have largely gone to capital owners and top executives rather than being distributed among workers.

2. **Labour Market Dynamics:** The shift from manufacturing to service-oriented and gig economy jobs has led to more precarious and lower-paying employment. These jobs often lack benefits and job security, contributing to wage stagnation.

3. **Minimum Wage Levels:** The federal minimum wage has not kept up with inflation. As a result, many workers earning minimum wage have seen their real incomes decline over time.

4. **Employer Practices:** Increased use of part-time and contract labour, wage suppression strategies, and anti-union practices by employers have contributed to stagnant wages.

Consequences of Income Inequality and Wage Stagnation

The consequences of rising income inequality and wage stagnation are profound and multifaceted, affecting both economic stability and social well-being:

1. **Economic Growth:** High levels of income inequality can hinder economic growth. When a large portion of the population experiences wage stagnation, consumer spending a key driver of economic growth is constrained.

2. **Social Mobility:** Income inequality limits social mobility, making it harder for individuals from lower-income backgrounds to improve their economic status. This can lead to entrenched poverty and a lack of opportunity.

3. **Health and Well-being:** Economic disparities contribute to differences in access to healthcare, education, and other essential services. Those at the lower end of the income spectrum often face worse health outcomes and reduced life expectancy.

4. **Political Stability:** Widening economic disparities can lead to political instability and social unrest. When people feel that the

economic system is unfair and opportunities are limited, trust in institutions erodes, and populist movements gain traction.

Addressing Income Inequality and Wage Stagnation

Addressing these issues requires a multifaceted approach involving policy changes, economic reforms, and social initiatives. Here are several potential solutions:

1. **Progressive Taxation:** Implementing a more progressive tax system, where higher earners pay a larger share of their income in taxes, can help reduce income inequality. Tax revenues can be used to fund social programs and investments in education, healthcare, and infrastructure.

2. **Minimum Wage Increases:** Raising the federal minimum wage to a living wage level can help lift millions of workers out of poverty and reduce wage stagnation. Indexing the minimum wage to inflation ensures that it keeps pace with the cost of living.

3. **Strengthening Unions:** Supporting labour unions and collective bargaining can empower workers to negotiate for better wages and working conditions. Policies that protect the right to organize and prevent anti-union practices are essential.

4. **Education and Training:** Investing in education and workforce development is crucial for addressing skill disparities. Expanding access to quality education, vocational training, and lifelong learning opportunities can help workers adapt to changing job markets and command higher wages.

5. **Affordable Healthcare and Childcare:** Reducing the financial burden of healthcare and childcare can increase disposable income for low- and middle-income families. Policies that ensure affordable access to these essential services can help reduce economic disparities.

6. **Corporate Responsibility:** Encouraging or mandating corporate practices that promote fair wages, benefits, and worker participation in decision-making can help address wage stagnation. This includes promoting pay transparency and linking executive compensation to broader workforce pay scales.

7. **Public Investment:** Government investment in infrastructure, research and development, and green energy can create high-paying jobs and stimulate economic growth. These investments can also address regional economic disparities by promoting development in underserved areas.

Political Implications for the 2024 Elections

Income inequality and wage stagnation are likely to be key issues in the 2024 elections, influencing voter preferences and shaping campaign strategies. Candidates will need to address these concerns convincingly to gain voter support:

1. **Voter Concerns:** Economic disparities and wage stagnation are tangible issues that affect millions of Americans. Voters are likely to prioritize candidates who propose effective solutions to these problems, making economic policy a critical battleground in the upcoming elections.

2. **Policy Proposals:** Candidates will need to present clear and practical plans to address income inequality and wage stagnation. This may include specific measures such as tax reforms, minimum wage increases, and investments in education and healthcare.

3. **Economic Messaging:** Effective communication about economic policy will be crucial. Candidates must explain how their policies will benefit ordinary Americans and provide relief from economic disparities. This involves not only addressing

immediate concerns but also presenting a vision for long-term economic stability and prosperity.

4. **Political Accountability:** The handling of economic issues will impact perceptions of political accountability. Voters will scrutinize the actions taken by current leaders and their effectiveness in addressing income inequality and wage stagnation. This could influence their decisions at the ballot box.

Income inequality and wage stagnation are critical issues that significantly impact the economic well-being and social cohesion of the United States. Understanding the causes, consequences, and potential solutions to these problems is essential for evaluating the policy proposals and platforms of candidates in the 2024 elections. Effective solutions will require a comprehensive approach, combining progressive taxation, minimum wage increases, education and training investments, and corporate responsibility. As voters head to the polls, their concerns about economic disparities will play a pivotal role in shaping the future direction of economic policy in the United States.

Federal Budget and National Debt

The federal budget and national debt are critical economic issues that influence the fiscal health of the United States and the well-being of its citizens. The federal budget outlines the government's spending priorities and revenue sources, while the national debt represents the accumulation of budget deficits over time. As the 2024 elections approach, these topics are likely to be central to political discourse, as policymakers and voters grapple with the implications of fiscal policy on economic stability, public services, and future generations. This chapter delves into the complexities of the federal budget and national debt, exploring their causes, consequences, and potential solutions.

Understanding the Federal Budget

The federal budget is an annual financial statement in which the government outlines its planned expenditures and expected revenues. The budget process involves several key steps:

1. **Budget Proposal:** The President submits a budget proposal to Congress, detailing spending priorities and revenue estimates for the upcoming fiscal year.

2. **Congressional Action:** Congress reviews the President's proposal, makes modifications, and passes budget resolutions. Appropriations committees then allocate funds to various government agencies and programs.

3. **Budget Execution:** Once approved, the budget is implemented, and government agencies begin spending according to the allocated funds.

The federal budget is divided into two main categories: discretionary spending and mandatory spending.

1. **Discretionary Spending:** This includes spending on programs that Congress must review and approve annually. Major categories include defence, education, transportation, and scientific research.

2. **Mandatory Spending:** This consists of expenditures required by law, such as Social Security, Medicare, and Medicaid. These programs operate on autopilot and do not require annual approval by Congress.

    Revenue sources for the federal budget primarily include individual income taxes, payroll taxes, corporate income taxes, and various other taxes and fees.

The National Debt

The national debt is the total amount of money that the federal government owes to creditors. It is the sum of all past budget deficits minus any surpluses. The national debt can be categorized into two types:

1. **Debt Held by the Public:** This includes Treasury securities held by individuals, corporations, state and local governments, foreign governments, and other entities outside the federal government.

2. **Intragovernmental Holdings:** This includes Treasury securities held by federal government trust funds, such as Social Security and Medicare.

   As of 2024, the national debt stands at approximately $30 trillion, reflecting decades of budget deficits. Managing the national debt involves balancing the need for borrowing to finance government operations with the goal of maintaining fiscal sustainability.

Causes of Budget Deficits and Rising National Debt

Several factors contribute to persistent budget deficits and the rising national debt:

1. **Economic Cycles:** During economic downturns, government revenues typically decline due to reduced income and corporate taxes, while expenditures on social safety net programs increase. This leads to larger deficits.

2. **Tax Cuts:** Significant tax cuts, such as those implemented during the Reagan and Trump administrations, reduce government revenue without corresponding cuts in spending, contributing to larger deficits.

3. **Increased Spending:** Major spending initiatives, such as defence expenditures, stimulus programs, and entitlement expansions, contribute to rising deficits. For example, the COVID-19 pandemic led to substantial increases in government spending on healthcare, unemployment benefits, and economic stimulus measures.

4. **Demographic Changes:** An aging population increases the demand for Social Security, Medicare, and other entitlement programs, putting additional pressure on the federal budget.

Consequences of High National Debt

High levels of national debt have several significant consequences for the economy and society:

1. **Interest Payments:** As the national debt grows, so do the government's interest obligations. Interest payments on the debt consume a larger portion of the federal budget, reducing the funds available for other priorities such as education, infrastructure, and social programs.

2. **Crowding Out:** When the government borrows heavily, it can crowd out private investment by driving up interest rates. Higher interest rates make it more expensive for businesses and individuals to borrow, potentially slowing economic growth.

3. **Fiscal Flexibility:** High debt levels limit the government's ability to respond to economic crises and other emergencies. With a significant portion of the budget already committed to debt servicing, there is less flexibility to increase spending or cut taxes when needed.

4. **Intergenerational Equity:** Rising national debt raises concerns about intergenerational equity. Future generations may face

higher taxes or reduced public services as they bear the burden of repaying the debt accumulated by previous generations.

Addressing Budget Deficits and National Debt

Addressing budget deficits and the national debt requires a combination of spending reforms, revenue enhancements, and economic growth strategies. Potential solutions include:

1. **Spending Reforms:** Identifying and implementing efficiencies in government spending can help reduce deficits. This may involve reforming entitlement programs to ensure their long-term sustainability, reducing unnecessary expenditures, and improving the efficiency of government operations.

2. **Tax Reforms:** Increasing revenues through tax reforms can help address budget deficits. Options include closing tax loopholes, increasing tax rates on higher incomes, and implementing new taxes on wealth or financial transactions.

3. **Economic Growth:** Promoting economic growth is crucial for improving the fiscal outlook. Policies that stimulate investment, innovation, and productivity can increase government revenues without raising tax rates. Investments in infrastructure, education, and research can support long-term economic growth.

4. **Bipartisan Cooperation:** Effective fiscal policy requires bipartisan cooperation and compromise. Policymakers must work together to develop sustainable solutions that balance the need for fiscal responsibility with the imperative to support economic growth and social well-being.

Political Implications for the 2024 Elections

The federal budget and national debt are likely to be central issues in the 2024 elections, influencing voter preferences and shaping campaign strategies. Candidates will need to address these concerns convincingly to gain voter support:

1. **Voter Concerns:** Voters are increasingly concerned about the fiscal health of the country and the potential consequences of high national debt. Candidates who propose credible solutions to manage the budget and reduce the debt are likely to resonate with fiscally conscious voters.

2. **Policy Proposals:** Candidates will need to present clear and practical plans to address budget deficits and the national debt. This may include specific measures such as spending reforms, tax increases, and policies to promote economic growth.

3. **Economic Messaging:** Effective communication about fiscal policy will be crucial. Candidates must explain how their policies will benefit ordinary Americans and ensure long-term economic stability. This involves not only addressing immediate concerns but also presenting a vision for sustainable fiscal management.

4. **Political Accountability:** The handling of fiscal issues will impact perceptions of political accountability. Voters will scrutinize the actions taken by current leaders and their effectiveness in managing the budget and debt. This could influence their decisions at the ballot box.

Chapter 3
Candidates Economic Platforms

The economic platforms of candidates in the 2024 US elections will play a crucial role in shaping voter decisions and the future direction of the country. As the nation grapples with key economic challenges, including inflation, income inequality, and national debt, voters are looking for clear, actionable plans that promise to address these issues effectively. This chapter explores the economic policies proposed by the major candidates, providing a comprehensive analysis of their approaches to taxation, healthcare, job creation, and more. By examining the distinct economic visions put forth by each candidate, this chapter aims to equip readers with the knowledge to make informed decisions at the ballot box. Understanding these platforms is essential for evaluating how each candidate plans to navigate the economic battleground and steer the nation towards prosperity.

Tax Reform Proposals

Tax reform is a critical component of the economic platforms presented by candidates in the 2024 US elections. The structure and fairness of the tax system impact economic growth, income distribution, and government revenues, which are essential for funding public services and addressing fiscal challenges. This chapter provides an in-depth analysis of the tax reform proposals from the major candidates, examining their approaches to individual and corporate taxes, tax credits, and incentives designed to stimulate economic activity and address social inequities.

Individual Income Taxes

Individual income tax reform is often at the forefront of candidates' economic agendas. Here are the major proposals from the leading candidates:

1. Progressive Taxation

Some candidates advocate for a more progressive tax system, where higher earners pay a larger percentage of their income in taxes. This approach aims to reduce income inequality and generate additional revenue for social programs. Proposals include:

- **Increased Marginal Tax Rates:** Raising the top marginal tax rate for the highest income brackets. For example, increasing the rate on incomes over $1 million to 39.6% or higher.

- **Wealth Taxes:** Introducing taxes on the net wealth of the ultra-rich. This could include annual taxes on assets above a certain threshold, such as $50 million.

- **Capital Gains and Dividends:** Taxing capital gains and dividends at the same rate as ordinary income for high earners, eliminating the preferential treatment these forms of income currently receive.

2. Tax Relief for Middle and Lower-Income Families

To alleviate the tax burden on middle and lower-income families, candidates propose various measures such as:

- **Expanded Standard Deduction:** Increasing the standard deduction to reduce taxable income for most taxpayers.

- **Enhanced Tax Credits:** Expanding tax credits like the Earned Income Tax Credit (EITC) and Child Tax Credit (CTC) to provide more substantial benefits to working families and help lift children out of poverty.

- **Adjusting Tax Brackets:** Raising the income thresholds for lower tax brackets to ensure more of middle-income earnings are taxed at lower rates.

Corporate Taxes

Corporate tax reform is another focal point, with candidates offering different visions for how to tax businesses:

1. Corporate Tax Rate Adjustments

Candidates are divided on the appropriate level for the corporate tax rate:

- **Rate Increases:** Some propose increasing the corporate tax rate from its current level of 21% to rates as high as 28% or more. The goal is to raise revenue from profitable corporations to fund public investments and reduce deficits.

- **Rate Reductions:** Others argue for maintaining or even lowering the corporate tax rate to encourage investment and economic growth. Proponents believe that a lower tax rate will make the US more competitive internationally and stimulate job creation.

2. Closing Loopholes and Ensuring Fair Share

Many candidates advocate for closing loopholes and ensuring that corporations pay their fair share of taxes:

- **Minimum Tax on Book Income:** Implementing a minimum tax based on the financial statement income (book income) reported by large corporations, preventing them from using tax loopholes to pay little or no taxes.

- **Global Minimum Tax:** Supporting international efforts to establish a global minimum tax rate for multinational corporations to curb tax avoidance through profit shifting to low-tax jurisdictions.

- **Eliminating Tax Breaks:** Phasing out or eliminating specific tax breaks and deductions that primarily benefit large corporations, such as deductions for executive compensation and certain depreciation methods.

Tax Credits and Incentives

Candidates propose various tax credits and incentives to promote economic activity, address social issues, and transition to a greener economy:

1. Green Energy and Environmental Initiatives

To combat climate change and promote renewable energy, candidates suggest:

- **Clean Energy Tax Credits:** Expanding tax credits for renewable energy projects, including solar, wind, and geothermal. This includes investment tax credits (ITCs) and production tax credits (PTCs) to incentivize clean energy development.

- **Electric Vehicle Incentives:** Enhancing tax credits for the purchase of electric vehicles (EVs) and investments in EV infrastructure, such as charging stations.

- **Energy Efficiency Improvements:** Providing tax incentives for businesses and homeowners to invest in energy-efficient upgrades and retrofits.

2. Economic and Social Equity

To address economic disparities and support disadvantaged communities, candidates propose:

- **Housing Tax Credits:** Expanding the Low-Income Housing Tax Credit (LIHTC) and introducing new credits to support affordable housing development and homeownership for low- and moderate-income families.

- **Education and Training:** Offering tax incentives for businesses that invest in employee training and education programs, particularly in underserved areas.

- **Healthcare Access:** Providing tax credits to reduce the cost of health insurance premiums and out-of-pocket expenses, especially for small businesses and low-income individuals.

3. Small Business Support

To foster entrepreneurship and support small businesses, candidates suggest:

- **Startup Tax Credits:** Introducing tax credits for new businesses to offset initial startup costs and encourage innovation.

- **Investment Incentives:** Expanding Section 179 expensing and bonus depreciation to allow small businesses to deduct the full cost of qualifying equipment and software in the year it is purchased.

- **Access to Capital:** Offering tax incentives for investments in small businesses, such as through Opportunity Zones and community development financial institutions (CDFIs).

Simplification and Compliance

Improving the simplicity and compliance of the tax system is another common theme among candidates:

1. Simplifying Tax Filing

Candidates propose measures to make tax filing easier for individuals and businesses:

- **Pre-Filled Tax Returns:** Introducing pre-filled tax returns for individuals with straightforward tax situations, reducing the burden of tax preparation.

- **Streamlining Deductions and Credits:** Simplifying the tax code by consolidating or eliminating redundant deductions and credits to make it easier for taxpayers to understand and comply with their tax obligations.

2. Enhanced Enforcement

To ensure that all taxpayers pay their fair share, candidates support increased enforcement:

- **Boosting IRS Funding:** Increasing funding for the Internal Revenue Service (IRS) to enhance tax enforcement, audit capabilities, and taxpayer services.

- **Cracking Down on Tax Evasion:** Implementing stricter penalties for tax evasion and aggressive tax avoidance schemes, particularly among high-income individuals and large corporations.

Political Implications for the 2024 Elections

Tax reform is a contentious issue with significant political implications. Voters are keenly interested in how proposed changes will affect their finances and the broader economy:

1. **Voter Concerns:** Tax policies directly impact voters' disposable income, savings, and economic opportunities. Candidates who can clearly articulate the benefits of their tax reform proposals and address voter concerns about fairness and economic impact are likely to gain support.

2. **Economic Messaging:** Effective communication about tax reform is crucial. Candidates must explain how their policies will foster economic growth, reduce inequality, and ensure fiscal responsibility. Voters need to understand how tax changes will affect them personally and contribute to national goals.

3. **Policy Feasibility:** Voters and analysts will scrutinize the feasibility of tax reform proposals. Candidates must provide detailed plans and realistic assessments of how they will implement and fund their proposed changes.

Tax reform is a central issue in the 2024 US elections, with significant implications for economic growth, income distribution, and government revenues. The candidates' proposals reflect different visions for how to achieve a fair and effective tax system. From progressive taxation and corporate tax adjustments to targeted tax credits and simplification measures, the range of ideas highlights the importance of tax policy in shaping the nation's economic future. As voters evaluate these proposals, they will consider their potential impact on their own finances and the broader economy, making tax reform a critical battleground in the upcoming elections.

Approaches to Healthcare Spending

Healthcare spending is a pivotal issue in the 2024 US elections, reflecting broader debates about the role of government, the effectiveness of market solutions, and the moral imperative to ensure access to healthcare for all citizens. The candidates' approaches to healthcare spending offer distinct visions for addressing these concerns. This chapter explores the various strategies proposed by major candidates, focusing on public versus private healthcare systems, cost control measures, and innovations aimed at improving healthcare delivery and outcomes.

Public vs. Private Healthcare Systems

The debate over the role of public versus private healthcare is central to the candidates' healthcare platforms. The spectrum of proposals ranges from expanding government-run programs to enhancing market-based solutions.

1. Medicare for All

Some candidates advocate for a single-payer system, often referred to as "Medicare for All." This approach involves expanding the existing Medicare program to cover all Americans, effectively eliminating private insurance.

- **Pros:** Proponents argue that Medicare for All would simplify the healthcare system, reduce administrative costs, and ensure universal coverage. By negotiating prices directly with providers, the government could potentially lower overall healthcare costs.

- **Cons:** Critics highlight the potential for increased government spending and taxation to fund the program. There are also concerns about the disruption to the current system, including the elimination of private insurance options and potential impacts on provider reimbursement rates.

2. Public Option

A more moderate approach involves introducing a public option, which would create a government-run health insurance plan to compete with private insurers.

- **Pros:** Supporters believe this would increase competition, drive down premiums, and expand coverage without completely overhauling the current system. It offers an additional choice for consumers while preserving private insurance.

- **Cons:** Opponents argue that a public option could still lead to increased government spending and may eventually drive private insurers out of the market if the public plan offers significantly lower premiums due to government subsidies.

3. Market-Based Reforms

On the other end of the spectrum, some candidates advocate for strengthening market-based solutions to improve efficiency and reduce costs in the healthcare system.

- **Pros:** Proponents argue that competition among private insurers and healthcare providers can drive innovation, improve quality, and reduce costs. Strategies include expanding Health Savings Accounts (HSAs), allowing insurance sales across state lines, and reducing regulatory burdens.

- **Cons:** Critics contend that market-based approaches do not adequately address issues of affordability and access, particularly for low-income individuals and those with pre-existing conditions. There is also concern that these reforms may not sufficiently control rising healthcare costs.

Cost Control Measures

Controlling healthcare costs is a priority for all candidates, given the significant burden healthcare spending places on the economy and individuals. Different strategies are proposed to achieve this goal:

1. **Drug Price Negotiation**

Many candidates propose allowing the federal government to negotiate drug prices directly with pharmaceutical companies, particularly for Medicare.

- **Pros:** Negotiation could lead to substantial cost savings for both the government and consumers. It could also reduce the out-of-pocket costs for prescription drugs.

- **Cons:** Opponents argue that this could stifle innovation by reducing the profits that fund research and development of new drugs. There is also concern about the potential for reduced access to certain medications if negotiations lead to fewer options being covered.

2. **Price Transparency**

Increasing price transparency in healthcare is another common proposal aimed at empowering consumers and fostering competition.

- **Pros:** Requiring hospitals and providers to disclose prices for procedures and services can help patients make more informed decisions and potentially lower costs by fostering competition.

- **Cons:** Critics argue that price transparency alone may not significantly impact costs without accompanying measures to address underlying price variations and the complexity of healthcare billing.

3. **Value-Based Care**

Shifting from fee-for-service to value-based care models is a strategy aimed at improving outcomes while controlling costs.

- **Pros:** Value-based care rewards providers for quality and efficiency rather than the volume of services delivered. This approach can lead to better patient outcomes and reduced costs by incentivizing preventive care and chronic disease management.

- **Cons:** Implementing value-based care requires significant changes to the current payment systems and healthcare delivery models. There are challenges in measuring and rewarding value accurately, and providers may face financial risks under these models.

4. **Administrative Simplification**

Reducing administrative costs and complexity is a priority for candidates aiming to make the healthcare system more efficient.

- **Pros:** Simplifying administrative processes, such as billing and insurance claims, can reduce overhead costs and free up resources for patient care. Streamlining regulations and standardizing procedures can also enhance efficiency.

- **Cons:** While administrative simplification can yield savings, it requires substantial coordination and cooperation across the healthcare system. There are concerns about the initial costs and disruption associated with implementing new administrative systems.

Innovations in Healthcare Delivery and Outcomes

Candidates also propose various innovations to improve healthcare delivery and outcomes, addressing both access and quality of care:

1. **Telehealth Expansion**

The COVID-19 pandemic accelerated the adoption of telehealth, and many candidates propose expanding its use permanently.

- **Pros:** Telehealth increases access to care, particularly in rural and underserved areas. It can also reduce healthcare costs by minimizing the need for in-person visits and allowing for more efficient management of chronic conditions.
- **Cons:** Challenges include ensuring equitable access to technology, maintaining patient privacy, and integrating telehealth with existing healthcare systems.

2. **Mental Health and Substance Abuse Services**

Addressing mental health and substance abuse is a priority, with candidates proposing increased funding and integration of these services into primary care.

- **Pros:** Enhanced access to mental health and substance abuse services can improve overall health outcomes and reduce long-term healthcare costs by preventing more severe conditions.
- **Cons:** There is a need for substantial investment in mental health infrastructure and workforce, and integrating these services with primary care can be complex.

3. **Health Equity Initiatives**

Candidates emphasize the importance of addressing health disparities and promoting equity in healthcare.

- **Pros:** Initiatives to improve access to care for marginalized communities, address social determinants of health, and promote culturally competent care can reduce disparities and improve population health.

- **Cons:** Achieving health equity requires comprehensive and sustained efforts across multiple sectors, including healthcare, education, housing, and employment. This can be resource-intensive and politically challenging.

Political Implications for the 2024 Elections

Healthcare spending is a deeply personal issue for voters, influencing their decisions and shaping campaign strategies:

1. **Voter Concerns:** Access to affordable, high-quality healthcare remains a top priority for many Americans. Candidates who can present clear, feasible solutions to control costs and improve access are likely to resonate with voters.

2. **Policy Proposals:** Detailed and actionable healthcare proposals are essential for gaining voter trust. Candidates need to explain how their plans will address the immediate concerns of affordability and access while ensuring long-term sustainability.

3. **Economic Messaging:** Effective communication about healthcare policies is crucial. Candidates must articulate how their proposals will impact not only individual health outcomes but also broader economic stability and growth.

4. **Political Accountability:** Voters will scrutinize the effectiveness of current and past leaders in managing healthcare issues. Candidates' records on healthcare policy and their ability to implement proposed reforms will be key factors in the elections.

Healthcare spending is a complex and multifaceted issue that will play a critical role in the 2024 US elections. The candidates' proposals reflect a range of approaches to managing costs, improving access, and ensuring quality care. From public versus private systems and cost control measures to innovations in healthcare delivery, the strategies outlined by the candidates offer voters a variety of visions for the future of healthcare in America. Understanding these proposals is essential for making informed decisions at the ballot box and shaping the nation's healthcare policy moving forward.

Plans for Infrastructure Investment

Infrastructure investment is a critical issue that has garnered significant attention in the 2024 US elections. The state of the nation's infrastructure—including transportation networks, energy systems, water supply, and broadband connectivity—directly impacts economic growth, public safety, and quality of life. Candidates propose various strategies for addressing infrastructure needs, with differing views on funding, priorities, and the role of government versus private sector involvement. This chapter explores the major candidates' infrastructure investment plans in detail, examining their approaches to transportation, energy, water, and digital infrastructure.

Transportation Infrastructure

Transportation infrastructure, including roads, bridges, public transit, and airports, is essential for economic activity and daily life. The candidates' proposals for transportation infrastructure investment focus on modernization, sustainability, and safety.

1. Roads and Bridges

Many candidates emphasize the need to repair and upgrade the nation's aging roads and bridges. Proposals include:

- **Increased Funding:** Advocating for significant increases in federal funding for the repair and maintenance of roads and bridges. This includes modernizing the Highway Trust Fund and ensuring sustainable long-term financing.

- **Public-Private Partnerships:** Encouraging public-private partnerships (PPPs) to leverage private investment in infrastructure projects. PPPs can provide additional capital and expertise, though they must be carefully managed to protect public interests.

- **Innovative Materials and Technologies:** Promoting the use of advanced materials and construction techniques to extend the lifespan of infrastructure and reduce maintenance costs. This includes investment in research and development of sustainable and resilient materials.

2. Public Transit

Enhancing public transit systems is a priority for many candidates, particularly in urban areas where congestion and pollution are major concerns.

- **Expansion and Modernization:** Proposals include expanding and modernizing transit networks, such as subways, buses, and light rail systems. Investment in transit infrastructure aims to improve accessibility, reduce travel times, and decrease carbon emissions.

- **Electrification:** Supporting the electrification of public transit fleets to reduce greenhouse gas emissions and reliance on fossil fuels. This includes funding for electric buses and trains, as well as charging infrastructure.

- **Affordability and Accessibility:** Ensuring public transit is affordable and accessible to all residents, including low-income communities and people with disabilities. This involves subsidies, fare reductions, and improved transit services in underserved areas.

3. **Airports and Ports**

Modernizing airports and ports is critical for maintaining the country's competitiveness in global trade and travel.

- **Airport Upgrades:** Proposals include upgrading airport facilities, improving air traffic control systems, and enhancing passenger experience. Investments aim to increase capacity, reduce delays, and support economic growth.

- **Port Infrastructure:** Enhancing port infrastructure to accommodate larger ships, improve logistics, and reduce congestion. This includes deepening harbors, upgrading cargo handling equipment, and improving intermodal connections to rail and road networks.

Energy Infrastructure

The transition to a sustainable and resilient energy infrastructure is a key component of the candidates' plans, reflecting the urgent need to address climate change and ensure energy security.

1. **Renewable Energy**

Expanding renewable energy capacity is a cornerstone of many candidates' infrastructure plans.

- **Investment in Solar and Wind:** Proposals include significant investments in solar and wind energy projects, both onshore and offshore. This involves funding for research, development, and deployment of renewable energy technologies.

- **Grid Modernization:** Modernizing the electric grid to accommodate renewable energy sources and enhance reliability. This includes upgrading transmission and distribution infrastructure, integrating smart grid technologies, and improving energy storage capabilities.

- **Community Energy Projects:** Supporting community-based renewable energy projects to promote local energy production and resilience. This includes grants and incentives for community solar, wind, and micro grid projects.

2. Energy Efficiency

Improving energy efficiency in buildings, transportation, and industry is a priority for reducing energy consumption and emissions.

- **Building Retrofits:** Proposals include funding for energy-efficient retrofits of residential, commercial, and public buildings. This involves improving insulation, heating and cooling systems, and lighting to reduce energy use.

- **Industrial Efficiency:** Promoting energy efficiency in industrial processes through grants, tax incentives, and technical assistance. This aims to reduce energy consumption and enhance competitiveness.

- **Energy-Efficient Transportation:** Investing in energy-efficient transportation options, including electric vehicles (EVs) and EV charging infrastructure. This includes subsidies for EV purchases and incentives for developing EV infrastructure.

3. Resilience and Security

Enhancing the resilience and security of energy infrastructure is critical for protecting against natural disasters, cyberattacks, and other threats.

- **Infrastructure Hardening:** Proposals include hardening critical energy infrastructure against extreme weather events and other hazards. This involves reinforcing power lines, substations, and pipelines to withstand damage.

- **Cybersecurity:** Investing in cybersecurity measures to protect energy infrastructure from cyber threats. This includes upgrading security protocols, conducting regular assessments, and enhancing coordination between government and industry.

Water Infrastructure

Ensuring a safe and reliable water supply is essential for public health, agriculture, and industry. The candidates' plans for water infrastructure focus on modernization, conservation, and climate resilience.

1. Water Supply and Treatment

Upgrading water supply and treatment infrastructure is a priority to ensure clean and safe drinking water.

- **Lead Pipe Replacement:** Proposals include funding for the replacement of lead pipes and other aging infrastructure to prevent contamination and ensure safe drinking water.

- **Water Treatment Facilities:** Investing in the modernization of water treatment facilities to improve water quality and compliance with environmental standards. This includes advanced treatment technologies and expanded capacity.

- **Rural Water Infrastructure:** Supporting water infrastructure projects in rural and underserved communities to ensure equitable access to clean water. This involves grants and low-interest loans for small and rural water systems.

2. Water Conservation

Promoting water conservation and efficient use of water resources is critical for sustainability.

- **Agricultural Efficiency:** Proposals include funding for water-efficient irrigation technologies and practices to reduce water use in agriculture. This aims to improve crop yields and sustainability.

- **Urban Conservation Programs:** Supporting urban water conservation programs, such as rebate programs for water-efficient appliances and fixtures, and public education campaigns on water conservation.

- **Leak Detection and Repair:** Investing in technologies and programs to detect and repair leaks in water distribution systems to reduce water loss and improve efficiency.

3. Climate Resilience

Enhancing the resilience of water infrastructure to climate change impacts is essential for long-term sustainability.

- **Flood Control and Management:** Proposals include funding for flood control infrastructure, such as levees, dams, and storm water management systems. This aims to protect communities from flooding and improve water management.

- **Drought Resilience:** Investing in infrastructure and programs to enhance drought resilience, such as reservoirs, desalination plants, and water recycling facilities. This aims to ensure reliable water supply during drought conditions.

- **Ecosystem Restoration:** Supporting ecosystem restoration projects to improve watershed health and resilience. This includes wetlands restoration, reforestation, and habitat protection.

Digital Infrastructure

Investing in digital infrastructure is crucial for ensuring connectivity, economic growth, and access to information.

1. Broadband Expansion

Expanding broadband access to underserved and rural areas is a priority for many candidates.

- **Rural Broadband:** Proposals include funding for the expansion of high-speed internet access in rural and underserved communities. This aims to bridge the digital divide and ensure equitable access to information and services.

- **Affordable Access:** Supporting programs to make broadband more affordable for low-income households, such as subsidies or sliding-scale pricing models.

- **5G Deployment:** Promoting the deployment of 5G networks to enhance connectivity and support technological innovation. This involves funding for infrastructure development and regulatory support.

2. Digital Literacy and Inclusion

Ensuring that all citizens have the skills and resources to benefit from digital technology is essential for equity.

- **Digital Literacy Programs:** Proposals include funding for digital literacy programs in schools, libraries, and community centers. This aims to equip individuals with the skills needed to use digital technology effectively.

- **Access to Devices:** Supporting initiatives to provide affordable access to digital devices, such as computers and tablets, particularly for students and low-income families.

3. **Cybersecurity**

Enhancing cybersecurity for critical digital infrastructure is essential for protecting against cyber threats.

- **Infrastructure Protection:** Investing in cybersecurity measures to protect critical infrastructure, such as power grids, financial systems, and communication networks. This includes upgrading security protocols and enhancing coordination between government and industry.
- **Cyber Workforce Development:** Supporting programs to develop a skilled cybersecurity workforce, including training and education initiatives.

Political Implications for the 2024 Elections

Infrastructure investment is a key issue that resonates with voters and shapes campaign strategies:

1. **Voter Concerns:** Voters are concerned about the state of infrastructure and its impact on daily life. Candidates who present clear and actionable plans for infrastructure investment are likely to gain support.
2. **Policy Proposals:** Detailed infrastructure proposals are essential for gaining voter trust. Candidates need to explain how their plans will address immediate needs and ensure long-term sustainability.
3. **Economic Messaging:** Effective communication about infrastructure policies is crucial. Candidates must articulate

how their proposals will create jobs, stimulate economic growth, and improve quality of life.

4. **Political Accountability:** Voters will scrutinize candidates' records on infrastructure investment and their ability to implement proposed reforms. Candidates' past performance

    Infrastructure investment is a critical issue that will significantly impact the 2024 US elections. The candidates' proposals reflect a range of approaches to addressing the nation's infrastructure needs, from transportation and energy to water and digital connectivity. Understanding these plans is essential for evaluating.

Chapter 4
The Role of the Federal Reserve

The Federal Reserve, often referred to as the Fed, plays a pivotal role in shaping the economic landscape of the United States. As the nation's central bank, the Fed is tasked with managing monetary policy to promote maximum employment, stable prices, and moderate long-term interest rates. Its decisions influence interest rates, inflation, and overall economic growth, affecting everything from mortgage rates to business investment. In the context of the 2024 elections, the Fed's policies and actions are under intense scrutiny as candidates' debate the best strategies for achieving economic stability and growth. This chapter explores the role of the Federal Reserve in the U.S. economy, examining its tools, decision-making processes, and the political and economic implications of its policies. Understanding the Fed's influence is essential for evaluating the economic platforms of the candidates and their potential impact on the nation's economic future.

Interest Rate Policies and Economic Growth

Interest rate policies are a fundamental tool used by the Federal Reserve (the Fed) to manage economic growth, control inflation, and stabilize the financial system. By influencing the cost of borrowing and the return on savings, the Fed's interest rate decisions have far-reaching implications for the economy. This section delves into how the Fed uses interest rate policies, their impact on economic growth, and the broader economic context within which these policies operate.

The Federal Reserve's Tools and Mechanisms

The Federal Reserve uses several key tools to influence interest rates and, by extension, economic growth:

1. **Federal Funds Rate:** The primary tool is the federal funds rate, which is the interest rate at which banks lend to each other overnight. Changes in the federal funds rate ripple through the economy, affecting other interest rates such as those on mortgages, auto loans, and business loans.

2. **Open Market Operations:** The Fed conducts open market operations by buying or selling government securities to influence the supply of money in the banking system. Buying securities injects money into the economy, lowering interest rates, while selling securities has the opposite effect.

3. **Discount Rate:** The discount rate is the interest rate the Fed charges banks for short-term loans. Changes in the discount rate can influence the cost of borrowing for banks, which in turn affects the interest rates they charge customers.

4. **Reserve Requirements:** By adjusting the amount of funds that banks must hold in reserve, the Fed can influence the amount of money available for lending. Lower reserve requirements increase the money supply and lower interest rates, while higher requirements do the opposite.

Impact on Economic Growth

Interest rate policies directly impact economic growth through several channels:

1. **Consumer Spending:** Lower interest rates reduce the cost of borrowing for consumers, encouraging spending on big-ticket items like homes and cars. Increased consumer spending boosts economic activity and contributes to growth.

2. **Business Investment:** Lower borrowing costs make it cheaper for businesses to finance new investments in equipment, facilities, and technology. This investment drives economic growth by increasing productive capacity and creating jobs.

3. **Housing Market:** Interest rates significantly affect mortgage rates. Lower mortgage rates make home buying more affordable, stimulating demand in the housing market, which in turn drives economic growth through increased construction activity and related services.

4. **Exports and Imports:** Interest rate policies can influence exchange rates. Lower interest rates tend to weaken the national currency, making exports cheaper and imports more expensive. This can boost domestic production and growth by improving the trade balance.

5. **Inflation Control:** By raising interest rates, the Fed can cool down an overheated economy, reducing inflationary pressures. Conversely, lowering interest rates can help stimulate economic activity during periods of low inflation or deflation.

Economic Context and Challenges

The effectiveness and impact of interest rate policies depend on the broader economic context. Several factors can influence how these policies play out:

1. **Economic Cycles:** During economic downturns, the Fed typically lowers interest rates to stimulate growth. Conversely, in periods of robust economic growth, the Fed may raise rates to prevent the economy from overheating and to keep inflation in check.

2. **Global Influences:** The U.S. economy is influenced by global economic conditions. For instance, if major trading partners are

experiencing slow growth or recession, it can dampen the impact of the Fed's interest rate cuts. Conversely, global economic booms can amplify the effects of Fed rate hikes.

3. **Financial Markets:** Interest rate changes can have immediate effects on financial markets. Lower rates generally boost stock prices by making bonds less attractive and reducing borrowing costs for companies. Higher rates can lead to market volatility as investors adjust their portfolios in response to changing returns on different assets.

4. **Consumer and Business Confidence:** The response of consumers and businesses to interest rate changes depends on their confidence in the economic outlook. If confidence is low, even significant rate cuts might not lead to increased spending and investment. Conversely, high confidence can amplify the effects of modest rate changes.

Recent Trends and the 2024 Election Context

In recent years, the Fed has faced unique challenges in setting interest rate policies. The COVID-19 pandemic led to unprecedented economic disruptions, prompting the Fed to lower interest rates to near-zero levels to support the economy. As the economy recovered, the Fed began to face new challenges, including rising inflation and supply chain disruptions.

Heading into the 2024 elections, the Fed's interest rate policies are a focal point of debate. Candidates discuss how best to balance the need for continued economic growth with the risks of inflation. Proposals range from maintaining accommodative policies to support job creation and investment, to tightening monetary policy to prevent runaway inflation and ensure long-term stability.

The Fed's Response to Economic Crises

The Federal Reserve, as the central bank of the United States, plays a crucial role in responding to economic crises. Its actions during such periods are aimed at stabilizing the financial system, supporting economic activity, and mitigating the negative impacts on households and businesses. This section delves into the strategies and tools employed by the Fed in response to economic crises, examining historical examples to illustrate its approaches and effectiveness.

Tools and Strategies for Crisis Management

The Fed has a range of tools and strategies at its disposal to respond to economic crises:

1. **Interest Rate Adjustments**

   - **Lowering the Federal Funds Rate:** In times of economic downturn, the Fed often cuts the federal funds rate to reduce borrowing costs and stimulate spending and investment. Lower interest rates make it cheaper for consumers and businesses to borrow money, which can boost economic activity.

   - **Zero Lower Bound:** During severe crises, the Fed may lower interest rates to near-zero levels, as seen during the 2008 financial crisis and the COVID-19 pandemic. When rates are near zero, the Fed must rely more on unconventional monetary policy tools.

2. **Quantitative Easing (QE)**

   - **Asset Purchases:** Quantitative easing involves the Fed purchasing long-term securities, such as government bonds and mortgage-backed securities, to inject liquidity into the financial system. This aims to lower long-term interest rates, support asset prices, and encourage lending and investment.

- **Market Stabilization:** By buying large amounts of securities, the Fed can help stabilize financial markets, ensuring that credit continues to flow to households and businesses.

3. **Emergency Lending Programs**

    - **Discount Window Lending:** The Fed can provide short-term loans to banks through the discount window, ensuring that they have the liquidity needed to meet customer withdrawals and lending demands.

    - **Special Lending Facilities:** During crises, the Fed may establish special lending facilities to support specific sectors or markets. For example, during the 2008 crisis, the Fed created the Term Auction Facility (TAF) to provide liquidity to banks, and during the COVID-19 pandemic, it introduced facilities like the Primary Market Corporate Credit Facility (PMCCF) to support corporate debt markets.

4. **Forward Guidance**

    - **Communicating Future Policy Intentions:** The Fed uses forward guidance to influence expectations about the future path of interest rates and monetary policy. Clear communication about future policy actions can help stabilize markets and guide economic decision-making.

5. **Regulatory and Supervisory Actions**

    - **Ensuring Financial Stability:** The Fed works to ensure the stability of the financial system by monitoring and regulating banks and other financial institutions. During crises, it may take actions to strengthen the resilience of the financial sector, such as stress testing banks to ensure they can withstand adverse conditions.

Historical Examples of Fed Responses

Examining the Fed's response to past economic crises provides insights into its strategies and their effectiveness:

1. **The 2008 Financial Crisis**

    - **Interest Rate Cuts:** The Fed rapidly cut the federal funds rate from 5.25% in September 2007 to near-zero by December 2008 to support the economy.

    - **Quantitative Easing:** The Fed launched several rounds of QE, purchasing trillions of dollars in securities to stabilize financial markets and promote economic recovery.

    - **Emergency Programs:** The Fed introduced numerous emergency lending programs, including the TAF, Term Securities Lending Facility (TSLF), and the Commercial Paper Funding Facility (CPFF), to provide liquidity and support credit markets.

    - **Forward Guidance:** The Fed provided forward guidance indicating that it would keep interest rates low for an extended period to support economic recovery.

2. **The COVID-19 Pandemic**

    - **Interest Rate Cuts:** In March 2020, the Fed swiftly cut the federal funds rate to near-zero in response to the economic impact of the pandemic.

    - **Quantitative Easing:** The Fed resumed large-scale asset purchases, buying Treasuries and mortgage-backed securities to support market functioning and provide liquidity.

- **Emergency Lending Facilities:** The Fed established a range of facilities, including the PMCCF, Secondary Market Corporate Credit Facility (SMCCF), and the Pay Check Protection Program Liquidity Facility (PPPLF), to support various segments of the economy.

- **Forward Guidance:** The Fed committed to maintaining low interest rates until substantial progress was made toward economic recovery, providing assurance to markets and investors.

Effectiveness and Challenges

The Fed's responses to economic crises have generally been effective in stabilizing financial markets, supporting economic activity, and mitigating the negative impacts of crises. However, these measures also come with challenges and potential drawbacks:

1. **Lagging Effects:** Monetary policy actions, such as interest rate cuts and QE, can take time to fully impact the economy. The delay between implementation and effect can complicate crisis management.

2. **Unintended Consequences:** Prolonged periods of low interest rates and large-scale asset purchases can lead to asset bubbles and financial imbalances. Additionally, there are concerns about the Fed's balance sheet expansion and the potential for future inflation.

3. **Coordination with Fiscal Policy:** The effectiveness of the Fed's actions often depends on coordination with fiscal policy. During crises, fiscal measures such as direct payments to individuals, unemployment benefits, and business support are crucial complements to monetary policy.

4. **Political Pressures:** The Fed operates independently, but it can face political pressures, especially during crises. Ensuring that its actions remain focused on economic stability and recovery rather than political considerations is essential.

The Federal Reserve's response to economic crises is a critical aspect of its role in the U.S. economy. Through interest rate adjustments, quantitative easing, emergency lending programs, and forward guidance, the Fed works to stabilize financial markets, support economic activity, and mitigate the impacts of crises. Historical examples, such as the 2008 financial crisis and the COVID-19 pandemic, illustrate the Fed's ability to adapt its strategies to address unprecedented challenges. Understanding the Fed's response mechanisms and their effectiveness is essential for evaluating its role in economic management and the broader implications for economic stability and growth.

Balancing Inflation and Unemployment

Balancing inflation and unemployment is one of the most critical and complex tasks faced by the Federal Reserve. This dual mandate, aimed at promoting maximum employment and stable prices, requires careful calibration of monetary policy. The relationship between inflation and unemployment is often described by the Phillips Curve, which suggests an inverse relationship between the two. However, real-world dynamics are more complex, and the Fed must navigate various economic conditions to achieve its objectives. This section explores the tools and strategies used by the Fed to balance inflation and unemployment, the challenges involved, and historical examples that highlight the Fed's approach.

Understanding the Trade-Off

The Phillips Curve posits that low unemployment can lead to higher inflation, as increased demand for goods and services pushes prices up. Conversely, high unemployment can lead to lower inflation or deflation, as reduced demand exerts downward pressure on prices. While this model provides a general framework, the real-world relationship between inflation and unemployment is influenced by multiple factors, including expectations, productivity, and global economic conditions.

1. **Demand-Pull Inflation:** Occurs when high demand for goods and services exceeds supply, leading to higher prices. Low unemployment can contribute to demand-pull inflation as more people have income to spend.

2. **Cost-Push Inflation:** Arises when the costs of production increase, leading businesses to raise prices to maintain profit margins. This can happen independently of unemployment levels.

The Fed's Tools for Balancing Inflation and Unemployment

The Federal Reserve employs several tools to manage inflation and unemployment, primarily through adjustments to the federal funds rate and open market operations:

1. **Interest Rate Adjustments:**

    - **Lowering Interest Rates:** In times of high unemployment, the Fed may lower the federal funds rate to stimulate economic activity. Lower interest rates reduce the cost of borrowing for consumers and businesses, encouraging spending and investment, which can lead to job creation.

    - **Raising Interest Rates:** To combat high inflation, the Fed may raise interest rates, making borrowing more expensive. This can cool off demand and reduce upward pressure on prices, but it may also slow economic growth and increase unemployment.

2. **Open Market Operations:** The Fed buys or sells government securities to influence the money supply and interest rates. Buying securities injects liquidity into the economy, lowering interest rates and stimulating growth, while selling securities has the opposite effect.

3. **Quantitative Easing (QE):** During severe economic downturns, the Fed may engage in QE, purchasing large quantities of long-term securities to lower long-term interest rates and encourage investment. This was notably used during the 2008 financial crisis and the COVID-19 pandemic.

4. **Forward Guidance:** By communicating its future policy intentions, the Fed can influence economic expectations. Clear guidance about the likely path of interest rates can help stabilize markets and guide consumer and business decision-making.

Challenges in Balancing Inflation and Unemployment

Achieving a balance between inflation and unemployment involves several challenges:

1. **Lagged Effects:** Monetary policy actions often have delayed effects on the economy. For instance, changes in interest rates may take several months to impact consumer spending and business investment fully. This lag complicates the timing and magnitude of policy adjustments.

2. **Expectations Management:** Inflation expectations play a crucial role in actual inflation outcomes. If businesses and consumers expect higher future inflation, they may adjust their prices and wages accordingly, creating a self-fulfilling prophecy. The Fed must manage these expectations through credible and consistent communication.

3. **Global Influences:** The U.S. economy is interconnected with the global economy. External factors, such as international trade dynamics, global commodity prices, and foreign monetary policies, can impact domestic inflation and employment. The Fed must consider these global influences when making policy decisions.

4. **Structural Changes:** Shifts in the economy, such as technological advancements and changes in labour market dynamics, can alter the relationship between inflation and unemployment. The Fed must adapt its strategies to account for these structural changes.

Historical Examples

1. **The 1970s Stagflation:** The 1970s presented a challenging period of stagflation, characterized by high inflation and high unemployment. Traditional monetary policy tools were less effective, leading to significant economic hardship. The Fed eventually raised interest rates sharply in the early 1980s to curb inflation, resulting in a severe recession but ultimately stabilizing prices.

2. **The Great Recession (2008-2009):** During the Great Recession, the Fed lowered the federal funds rate to near-zero levels and implemented QE to support economic recovery. These measures helped reduce unemployment, but inflation remained low, demonstrating the complexities of the inflation-unemployment trade-off in different economic contexts.

3. **COVID-19 Pandemic:** The pandemic caused unprecedented economic disruption, leading the Fed to take aggressive actions, including cutting interest rates to near-zero and launching extensive QE programs. These measures aimed to support economic activity and prevent a deflationary spiral, contributing

to a relatively quick rebound in employment, though inflationary pressures emerged as the economy recovered.

Balancing inflation and unemployment is a delicate and complex task for the Federal Reserve. Through its tools of interest rate adjustments, open market operations, quantitative easing, and forward guidance, the Fed seeks to navigate the trade-offs between these two critical economic indicators. Historical examples highlight the challenges and nuances of this balancing act, demonstrating that the relationship between inflation and unemployment is influenced by various factors and requires adaptive and responsive policymaking. As the economy evolves, the Fed's ability to manage these dual objectives remains crucial for maintaining economic stability and promoting sustained growth.

Chapter 5
Taxation and Fiscal Policy Debates

Taxation and fiscal policy are pivotal issues in shaping the economic landscape and are at the heart of political debates, particularly in the lead-up to the 2024 US elections. These policies determine how the government collects and allocates resources, influencing everything from economic growth to income inequality. Candidates propose a wide array of strategies, reflecting their visions for addressing fiscal challenges and promoting prosperity. Key topics include progressive versus regressive taxation, corporate tax policies, and government spending priorities. Understanding the nuances of these debates is crucial for voters as they consider how different approaches will impact their lives and the nation's future. This chapter explores the core arguments and proposals surrounding taxation and fiscal policy, providing a comprehensive overview of the competing visions that will shape the economic discourse in the 2024 elections.

Progressive vs. Regressive Taxation

Taxation is a fundamental aspect of fiscal policy, shaping the way governments generate revenue to fund public services and infrastructure. Two primary approaches to taxation are progressive and regressive taxation, each with distinct impacts on income distribution, economic behavior, and social equity. This section delves into the principles, advantages, and disadvantages of progressive and regressive taxation, examining how these approaches influence economic and social outcomes.

Progressive Taxation

Definition and Principles:

Progressive taxation is based on the principle that individuals and entities with higher incomes should pay a larger percentage of their income in taxes compared to those with lower incomes. This approach is designed to reduce income inequality by redistributing wealth from the more affluent to those with lower incomes.

1. **Tax Brackets:** Progressive tax systems typically use tax brackets, where income is divided into segments, each taxed at progressively higher rates. For example, in the U.S., federal income tax rates increase with income levels, ranging from 10% for the lowest bracket to 37% for the highest bracket.

2. **Effective Tax Rates:** Under a progressive system, the effective tax rate the actual percentage of income paid in taxes—rises with income. This ensures that higher earners contribute a larger share of their income to government revenues.

Advantages:

1. **Equity and Fairness:** Progressive taxation is considered more equitable because it places a heavier burden on those who can afford to pay more. It aims to reduce income disparities and provide greater financial support for low- and middle-income households.

2. **Revenue Generation:** By taxing higher incomes at higher rates, progressive taxation can generate significant government revenue. This revenue can be used to fund essential public services such as education, healthcare, and social safety nets, benefiting society as a whole.

3. **Economic Stability:** Progressive taxes can help stabilize the economy by reducing disposable income disparities. Higher-

income individuals are less likely to spend all their income, so taxing them more heavily can redistribute purchasing power to lower-income individuals who are more likely to spend their income, boosting demand and economic activity.

Disadvantages:

1. **Economic Disincentives:** Critics argue that high marginal tax rates on high incomes can discourage investment, entrepreneurship, and work effort. If individuals feel that a significant portion of their additional earnings will be taxed away, they may be less motivated to earn more.

2. **Complexity and Compliance:** Progressive tax systems can be complex, with multiple brackets and deductions. This complexity can lead to higher administrative costs and compliance burdens for both taxpayers and the government.

3. **Potential for Tax Avoidance:** Higher tax rates on high incomes can incentivize tax avoidance strategies, such as using loopholes, deductions, or shifting income to lower-tax jurisdictions. This can undermine the effectiveness of progressive taxation.

Regressive Taxation

Definition and Principles:

Regressive taxation imposes a higher relative burden on low-income individuals compared to high-income individuals. In a regressive tax system, the tax rate decreases as the taxable amount increases, leading to lower-income earners paying a higher proportion of their income in taxes.

1. **Flat Taxes:** Some regressive taxes, such as flat taxes, apply the same tax rate to all taxpayers regardless of income level. While

the rate is constant, the tax burden is heavier on those with lower incomes.

2. **Consumption Taxes:** Sales taxes and excise taxes are often regressive because they apply uniformly to goods and services. Since lower-income individuals spend a larger proportion of their income on consumption, these taxes disproportionately affect them.

Advantages:

1. **Simplicity:** Regressive taxes, such as sales taxes, are relatively simple to administer and comply with. They are straightforward to collect and do not require complex calculations or multiple tax brackets.

2. **Broad-Based Revenue:** Consumption taxes can generate substantial revenue from a broad base of taxpayers. Everyone who purchases goods and services contributes to the tax revenue, ensuring a steady income stream for the government.

3. **Economic Efficiency:** Some argue that regressive taxes are less likely to distort economic behavior. Since they do not penalize higher incomes, they may encourage savings, investment, and economic growth.

Disadvantages:

1. **Inequity:** Regressive taxation is often criticized for being unfair to low-income individuals. By placing a heavier relative burden on those with lower incomes, it can exacerbate income inequality and financial hardship for the most vulnerable populations.

2. **Reduced Disposable Income:** Regressive taxes reduce the disposable income of lower-income households, limiting their ability to spend on essential goods and services. This can

negatively impact their standard of living and economic mobility.

3. **Social Impact:** Higher tax burdens on low-income individuals can lead to increased reliance on social safety nets and public assistance programs. This can strain government resources and reduce the overall effectiveness of fiscal policy.

Balancing Progressive and Regressive Taxation

Most modern tax systems incorporate elements of both progressive and regressive taxation to balance equity and efficiency. For example, a country might use a progressive income tax system alongside regressive sales taxes. The goal is to create a balanced approach that generates adequate revenue while minimizing economic distortions and ensuring fairness.

1. **Tax Credits and Deductions:** To mitigate the regressive effects of consumption taxes, governments often provide tax credits or deductions targeted at low-income households. These measures can help offset the disproportionate burden of regressive taxes.

2. **Comprehensive Fiscal Policy:** Effective fiscal policy requires a comprehensive approach that considers the combined impact of various taxes and public expenditures. By carefully designing tax policies and public spending programs, governments can promote both economic growth and social equity.

   Progressive and regressive taxation represent two distinct approaches to generating government revenue, each with its own set of advantages and disadvantages. Progressive taxation aims to reduce income inequality and provide a fairer distribution of the tax burden, while regressive taxation offers simplicity and economic efficiency but can exacerbate inequality. A balanced and well-designed tax system that incorporates elements of both approaches can help achieve fiscal sustainability, economic growth, and social equity. As the 2024 US elections approach, understanding these taxation principles and their implications will be crucial for voters evaluating the fiscal policies of different candidates.

Corporate Tax Policies

Corporate tax policies are a significant aspect of fiscal policy, influencing business behavior, investment decisions, and economic growth. These policies determine how much businesses pay in taxes on their profits and can vary widely depending on the political and economic priorities of a government. As the 2024 US elections approach, corporate tax policies are a major topic of debate among candidates, reflecting differing views on how to balance revenue generation, economic competitiveness, and equity. This section explores the principles, advantages, and disadvantages of various corporate tax policies, and examines the implications of these policies for the broader economy.

Principles of Corporate Taxation

Corporate tax policies are designed to generate revenue for the government while influencing business practices and economic activity. The key principles of corporate taxation include:

1. **Revenue Generation:** Corporate taxes are a significant source of revenue for the government, funding public services, infrastructure, and social programs.

2. **Economic Competitiveness:** Tax policies can impact the attractiveness of a country as a location for business investment. Lower corporate tax rates can make a country more competitive, attracting foreign investment and encouraging domestic businesses to expand.

3. **Equity and Fairness:** Corporate tax policies aim to ensure that businesses contribute their fair share to public finances. This involves addressing tax avoidance and ensuring that profitable corporations pay taxes commensurate with their earnings.

4. **Economic Efficiency:** Effective corporate tax policies seek to minimize economic distortions and encourage productive investment while avoiding excessive burdens that could stifle business activity.

Approaches to Corporate Taxation

Different approaches to corporate taxation reflect varying priorities and economic philosophies:

1. **Flat Corporate Tax Rates:**

    - **Definition:** A flat corporate tax rate imposes the same tax rate on all corporate profits, regardless of the amount.

    - **Advantages:** Simplicity and predictability are key benefits of flat tax rates. They are easy to administer and understand, reducing compliance costs for businesses.

    - **Disadvantages:** Flat tax rates do not account for the varying abilities of businesses to pay taxes. They may be perceived as less equitable since large, highly profitable corporations pay the same rate as smaller businesses.

2. **Graduated Corporate Tax Rates:**

    - **Definition:** Graduated tax rates impose higher tax rates on higher levels of corporate profit.

    - **Advantages:** This approach can be more equitable, as it ensures that larger, more profitable corporations pay a higher percentage of their income in taxes. It can also generate more revenue from businesses that are better able to afford it.

- **Disadvantages:** Graduated tax rates can add complexity to the tax system, increasing compliance costs. They may also discourage business expansion by penalizing higher profits.

3. **Minimum Corporate Tax:**

    - **Definition:** A minimum corporate tax sets a floor on the amount of tax a corporation must pay, regardless of deductions and credits.

    - **Advantages:** This approach can prevent profitable corporations from using loopholes to reduce their tax liability to zero. It ensures a baseline level of tax contribution from all businesses.

    - **Disadvantages:** Implementing a minimum tax can be complex and may create compliance challenges. It may also discourage the use of legitimate tax incentives aimed at encouraging investment and innovation.

Corporate Tax Incentives

Governments often use tax incentives to promote specific economic activities:

1. **Research and Development (R&D) Credits:**

    - **Purpose:** R&D tax credits incentivize businesses to invest in research and development, fostering innovation and technological advancement.

    - **Advantages:** Encouraging R&D can lead to new products, services, and processes that drive economic growth and competitiveness.

- **Disadvantages:** R&D credits can be costly and may be disproportionately utilized by larger corporations with the resources to invest heavily in research.

2. **Investment Incentives:**
    - **Purpose:** Investment incentives, such as accelerated depreciation and investment tax credits, encourage businesses to invest in capital assets like machinery, equipment, and infrastructure.
    - **Advantages:** These incentives can stimulate economic growth by promoting business expansion and job creation.
    - **Disadvantages:** They can lead to revenue losses for the government and may favor capital-intensive industries over others.

3. **Location-Based Incentives:**
    - **Purpose:** These incentives aim to attract businesses to specific areas, such as economically distressed regions or enterprise zones.
    - **Advantages:** Location-based incentives can promote regional economic development and reduce geographic inequalities.
    - **Disadvantages:** They can distort economic activity by encouraging businesses to relocate for tax benefits rather than operational efficiency.

Addressing Tax Avoidance and Evasion

Corporate tax policies must also address tax avoidance and evasion:

1. **International Tax Coordination:**

    - **Definition:** Cooperation among countries to harmonize tax policies and combat base erosion and profit shifting (BEPS).

    - **Advantages:** International coordination can reduce opportunities for tax avoidance by multinational corporations and ensure a fairer distribution of tax revenues.

    - **Disadvantages:** Achieving international consensus can be challenging, and countries may resist changes that reduce their competitive advantages.

2. **Tax Transparency and Reporting:**

    - **Definition:** Requirements for corporations to disclose detailed financial and tax information.

    - **Advantages:** Transparency measures can deter aggressive tax planning and allow governments to better assess and address tax risks.

    - **Disadvantages:** Compliance costs can be significant, and businesses may resist disclosing sensitive information.

3. **Anti-Avoidance Rules:**

    - **Definition:** Legal provisions designed to prevent tax avoidance strategies that exploit loopholes in the tax code.

    - **Advantages:** Anti-avoidance rules can protect the integrity of the tax system and ensure that businesses pay their fair share of taxes.

- **Disadvantages:** These rules can add complexity to the tax system and may require significant resources to enforce effectively.

  Corporate tax policies are a crucial element of fiscal policy, with significant implications for economic growth, equity, and government revenue. Various approaches, including flat and graduated tax rates, minimum taxes, and targeted incentives, reflect differing priorities and economic philosophies. Addressing tax avoidance and evasion through international coordination, transparency measures, and anti-avoidance rules is essential for maintaining the integrity of the tax system. As the 2024 US elections approach, understanding the nuances of these policies and their potential impacts is vital for voters and policymakers alike.

Government Spending Priorities

Government spending priorities reflect a nation's economic, social, and political goals, influencing the distribution of resources, economic growth, and the well-being of its citizens. As the 2024 US elections approach, candidates propose various strategies for allocating federal funds, addressing issues such as infrastructure, healthcare, education, defence, and social welfare. Understanding these spending priorities is crucial for evaluating their potential impact on the economy and society.

Infrastructure Investment

Infrastructure is a critical area of government spending, essential for economic growth and public welfare. Investment in infrastructure includes funding for transportation networks, utilities, and public facilities.

1. **Transportation Networks:**

   - **Roads and Bridges:** Maintenance and upgrading of highways, bridges, and local roads ensure efficient transportation and reduce the economic costs of traffic congestion and vehicle damage.

   - **Public Transit:** Expanding and modernizing public transit systems can reduce traffic congestion, lower emissions, and provide affordable transportation options, particularly in urban areas.

   - **Airports and Ports:** Investing in airports and ports enhances trade and travel efficiency, supporting economic growth and international competitiveness.

2. **Utilities and Public Facilities:**

   - **Water and Sewage Systems:** Upgrading aging water and sewage systems ensures access to clean water and prevents environmental contamination.

   - **Energy Infrastructure:** Modernizing the energy grid and investing in renewable energy sources can enhance energy security, reduce environmental impact, and support sustainable economic growth.

   - **Public Buildings:** Maintaining and upgrading schools, hospitals, and government buildings ensures they remain functional and safe for public use.

Healthcare Spending

Healthcare is a major component of government spending, impacting public health and economic productivity. Candidates propose different approaches to funding healthcare, ranging from expanding public programs to promoting private sector solutions.

Medicare and Medicaid:

- **Medicare:** Expanding Medicare coverage to include more services or lower the eligibility age can provide broader access to healthcare for older adults and reduce financial burdens.

- **Medicaid:** Increasing funding for Medicaid can help states provide healthcare to low-income individuals and families, improving health outcomes and reducing inequality.

Public Health Initiatives:

- **Preventive Care:** Investing in preventive care programs, such as vaccinations and screenings, can reduce the long-term costs of treating chronic diseases.

- **Mental Health Services:** Expanding access to mental health services can improve overall health outcomes and reduce costs associated with untreated mental health conditions.

- **Substance Abuse Programs:** Funding substance abuse prevention and treatment programs can reduce healthcare costs, improve public safety, and enhance quality of life.

Education Funding

Education is a priority for government spending, essential for economic growth and social mobility. Candidates propose various strategies to fund education, from early childhood through higher education.

1. **Early Childhood Education:**

    - **Pre-K Programs:** Investing in universal pre-kindergarten programs can improve educational outcomes and long-term economic productivity.

- **Childcare Support:** Providing affordable, high-quality childcare supports working families and promotes early childhood development.

2. **K-12 Education:**

    - **School Funding:** Ensuring equitable funding for public schools can reduce disparities in educational outcomes and support student achievement.
    - **Teacher Salaries:** Increasing teacher salaries can attract and retain qualified educators, improving the quality of education.

3. **Higher Education:**

    - **Tuition Assistance:** Expanding grants and scholarships can make higher education more accessible and reduce student debt burdens.
    - **Community Colleges:** Investing in community colleges and vocational training programs can provide affordable pathways to employment and support workforce development.

Defence and Security

Defence and security are significant areas of government spending, aimed at protecting national interests and ensuring public safety.

1. **Military Funding:**

    - **Modernization:** Investing in modernizing military equipment and technology ensures that the armed forces remain capable and prepared for future threats.

- **Personnel Support:** Providing adequate support for military personnel, including healthcare, housing, and education, ensures a high-quality, ready force.

2. **Homeland Security:**

    - **Border Security:** Funding for border security and immigration enforcement aims to protect national sovereignty and manage immigration flows.

    - **Cybersecurity:** Investing in cybersecurity measures protects critical infrastructure and sensitive information from cyber threats.

Social Welfare Programs

Social welfare programs are designed to support vulnerable populations and reduce poverty, impacting economic stability and social equity.

1. **Social Security:**

    - **Sustainability:** Ensuring the long-term sustainability of Social Security involves managing benefits and funding to support retirees and disabled individuals.

    - **Benefit Increases:** Proposals to increase Social Security benefits aim to reduce poverty among seniors and improve their quality of life.

2. **Unemployment Insurance:**

    - **Extended Benefits:** Providing extended unemployment benefits during economic downturns supports individuals who have lost their jobs and stimulates economic activity.

- **Job Training:** Funding job training and reemployment programs helps unemployed individuals acquire new skills and return to work.

3. **Food Assistance:**

    - **SNAP:** Increasing funding for the Supplemental Nutrition Assistance Program (SNAP) ensures that low-income families have access to nutritious food.
    - **School Meals:** Expanding free and reduced-price school meal programs can reduce child hunger and support academic achievement.

Balancing Priorities

Balancing spending priorities involves trade-offs and difficult decisions. Policymakers must consider the immediate and long-term impacts of their choices, aiming to promote economic growth, social equity, and fiscal sustainability. Effective fiscal policy requires careful assessment of needs, benefits, and costs, ensuring that government spending supports overall national goals.

Government spending priorities reflect the values and goals of a nation, influencing economic growth, social equity, and public welfare. As the 2024 US elections approach, understanding the candidates' proposed spending strategies in areas such as infrastructure, healthcare, education, defence, and social welfare is crucial for voters. These priorities will shape the future direction of the country, determining how resources are allocated and addressing the pressing challenges facing society.

Chapter 6

Healthcare Economics

Healthcare economics is a critical area of study that examines the allocation of resources within the healthcare system and the impact of these allocations on public health, economic stability, and overall societal well-being. As healthcare costs continue to rise and access to quality care remains a pressing issue, the economic dimensions of healthcare have become central to policy debates and electoral platforms. This chapter delves into the complex interplay between economic principles and healthcare, exploring topics such as the cost of healthcare delivery, the economic implications of healthcare policies, and the challenges of financing and regulating the healthcare system. With the 2024 US elections approaching, understanding healthcare economics is essential for evaluating the viability and impact of the candidates' proposals. This chapter aims to provide a comprehensive overview of how economic factors influence healthcare decisions, the distribution of resources, and the pursuit of equitable and efficient healthcare solutions.

The Cost of Universal Healthcare

Universal healthcare aims to provide comprehensive health coverage to all individuals, regardless of income, employment status, or health condition. While the concept of universal healthcare is widely supported for its potential to improve health outcomes and ensure equitable access to medical services, the cost of implementing such a system is a major point of contention. This section explores the various costs associated with universal healthcare, including direct financial expenditures, potential savings, and broader economic implications.

Direct Financial Expenditures

Implementing universal healthcare requires substantial upfront and ongoing financial investments. These costs include:

1. **Healthcare Services:** Universal healthcare systems must cover a wide range of medical services, from primary care and preventive services to specialist treatments and surgeries. Funding these services involves significant expenditure on healthcare providers, facilities, and medical equipment.

2. **Administrative Costs:** While universal healthcare can streamline administrative processes, transitioning to a new system incurs significant costs. These include establishing new administrative bodies, integrating existing systems, and managing the transition for patients and providers.

3. **Insurance Coverage:** Universal healthcare systems often involve government-provided or subsidized insurance plans. Funding these plans requires considerable public investment, covering premiums, co-pays, and other out-of-pocket expenses for millions of individuals.

4. **Infrastructure Development:** Expanding healthcare infrastructure to meet increased demand is essential. This involves building new hospitals and clinics, upgrading existing facilities, and ensuring adequate supply of medical professionals.

Potential Savings

Proponents of universal healthcare argue that despite the high initial costs, the system can lead to significant long-term savings:

1. **Reduced Administrative Costs:** Universal healthcare systems can simplify administrative processes by reducing the complexity associated with multiple insurance providers and billing systems. This can lead to lower administrative costs for both healthcare providers and the government.

2. **Preventive Care and Early Intervention:** By providing universal access to preventive care and early treatment, healthcare systems can reduce the incidence of chronic diseases and avoid costly emergency interventions. Early diagnosis and management of conditions can prevent complications and reduce overall healthcare costs.

3. **Negotiated Pricing:** Governments in universal healthcare systems often negotiate prices for drugs, medical devices, and services on behalf of the entire population. This bulk purchasing power can lead to lower prices and substantial cost savings compared to fragmented, market-based systems.

4. **Improved Health Outcomes:** Healthier populations contribute to economic productivity. Universal healthcare can lead to improved health outcomes, reducing absenteeism, increasing workforce productivity, and lowering long-term disability and social welfare costs.

Broader Economic Implications

The implementation of universal healthcare has significant economic implications beyond direct costs and savings:

1. **Taxation and Public Spending:** Funding universal healthcare typically requires increased public spending, which is often financed through higher taxes. While this can be politically challenging, the economic benefits of a healthier population can offset some of the fiscal impacts.

2. **Economic Security:** Universal healthcare can enhance economic security for individuals and families by reducing the financial burden of medical expenses. This can lead to increased disposable income and consumer spending, stimulating economic growth.

3. **Labour Market Effects:** Universal healthcare can influence the labour market by decoupling health insurance from employment. This can increase labour mobility, reduce job lock (where individuals stay in jobs primarily for health benefits), and encourage entrepreneurship.

4. **Healthcare Industry Dynamics:** The shift to a universal healthcare system can impact the healthcare industry, including insurance companies, pharmaceutical firms, and healthcare providers. While some sectors may face reduced profitability, others may benefit from increased demand and stable funding.

The cost of universal healthcare encompasses a range of direct financial expenditures, potential savings, and broader economic impacts. While the initial investment is substantial, the long-term benefits, including reduced administrative costs, improved health outcomes, and enhanced economic security, can make universal healthcare a sustainable and equitable solution. As the 2024 US elections approach, understanding these costs and benefits is crucial for evaluating the feasibility and impact of proposed healthcare reforms. Universal healthcare promises to address critical issues of access and affordability, but careful consideration of its economic implications is essential for successful implementation.

Impact of Healthcare Policies on Small Businesses

Healthcare policies significantly affect small businesses, influencing their financial stability, employee benefits, and overall competitiveness. As healthcare costs continue to rise, the impact of these policies becomes a crucial consideration for small business owners and policymakers alike. This section examines how various healthcare policies affect small businesses, exploring both the challenges and potential benefits.

Financial Implications

1. **Cost of Providing Health Insurance:**

    - **Premiums and Administrative Costs:** Small businesses often face higher health insurance premiums compared to larger firms due to a smaller risk pool. Additionally, administrative costs for managing health benefits can be proportionally higher, straining financial resources.

    - **Cost Variability:** Unlike larger corporations, small businesses are less able to absorb unexpected increases in healthcare costs, such as sudden spikes in premiums or medical claims. This unpredictability can impact budgeting and financial planning.

2. **Tax Credits and Subsidies:**

    - **Affordable Care Act (ACA) Provisions:** The ACA introduced tax credits for small businesses that provide health insurance to their employees. These credits can offset some of the costs, making it more feasible for small businesses to offer health benefits.

    - **Public Policy Proposals:** Future healthcare policies may include additional subsidies or tax incentives aimed at reducing the financial burden on small businesses, promoting wider adoption of employer-sponsored health insurance.

Employee Recruitment and Retention

1. **Competitive Benefits:**

   - **Attracting Talent:** Offering health insurance is a key factor in attracting and retaining skilled employees. Small businesses that provide comprehensive health benefits can compete more effectively with larger firms for top talent.

   - **Employee Loyalty and Productivity:** Health benefits contribute to employee well-being and job satisfaction, leading to higher productivity and reduced turnover. Small businesses that offer health insurance may see improvements in employee morale and loyalty.

2. **Impact of Mandates:**

   - **Employer Mandates:** Policies requiring businesses to provide health insurance can have mixed effects on small businesses. While they ensure that more employees receive coverage, they can also impose financial and administrative burdens on employers.

   - **Exemptions and Thresholds:** Many healthcare policies, including the ACA, provide exemptions or different requirements for small businesses based on their size. These measures are intended to balance the need for employee coverage with the financial capacity of small firms.

Operational and Strategic Considerations

1. **Health Insurance Marketplaces:**

   - **SHOP Marketplaces:** The Small Business Health Options Program (SHOP) marketplaces created by the ACA allow small businesses to compare and purchase health insurance plans. These marketplaces aim to increase transparency and competition, potentially lowering costs.

- **Plan Selection and Administration:** Navigating health insurance options can be complex for small business owners. Simplified enrolment processes and assistance with plan selection can reduce administrative burdens and help businesses find suitable coverage.

2. **Alternative Health Benefits:**

- **Health Reimbursement Arrangements (HRAs):** HRAs allow small businesses to reimburse employees for medical expenses or individual health insurance premiums. These arrangements provide flexibility and can be a cost-effective alternative to traditional group health insurance.

- **Wellness Programs:** Implementing wellness programs can promote employee health and reduce healthcare costs over time. Small businesses can benefit from lower insurance premiums and improved employee productivity through preventive care initiatives.

Regulatory and Policy Environment

1. **Compliance Challenges:**

- **Regulatory Complexity:** Keeping up with changing healthcare regulations can be challenging for small businesses. Compliance requires time, expertise, and resources that may be limited in small firms.

- **Support and Guidance:** Government agencies and industry associations can provide valuable support and guidance to help small businesses navigate healthcare regulations. Simplified compliance requirements and clear communication can reduce the administrative burden.

2. **Future Policy Developments:**

    - **Universal Healthcare Proposals:** Discussions about universal healthcare or public options could significantly impact small businesses. These policies could alleviate the burden of providing health insurance, but may also involve changes in tax structures or employer contributions.

    - **Innovative Health Solutions:** Policymakers are exploring innovative solutions to make healthcare more affordable and accessible. Proposals such as Medicare for All or expanded public health options could reshape the landscape for small business healthcare provision.

    Healthcare policies have a profound impact on small businesses, influencing their financial health, competitiveness, and ability to attract and retain employees. While providing health insurance can be a significant expense, it also offers considerable benefits in terms of employee satisfaction and productivity. Policymakers must consider the unique challenges faced by small businesses and strive to create a balanced regulatory environment that promotes affordable, accessible healthcare without imposing undue burdens. As the 2024 US elections approach, understanding the implications of healthcare policies on small businesses is essential for informed decision-making and effective advocacy.

Public vs. Private Healthcare Systems

The debate between public and private healthcare systems is a central issue in health policy, reflecting differing views on how to best provide and finance medical care. Each system has its own advantages and disadvantages, influencing access to care, cost efficiency, quality of services, and overall health outcomes. This section explores the key characteristics, benefits, and challenges of both public and private healthcare systems.

Public Healthcare Systems

Characteristics:

Public healthcare systems are primarily funded and administered by the government. They aim to provide universal coverage, ensuring that all citizens have access to necessary medical services regardless of their ability to pay. Key features include:

1. **Universal Coverage:** Public systems strive to cover all residents, offering a standardized package of essential health services.

2. **Government Funding:** These systems are typically financed through taxes, which fund healthcare services directly.

3. **Regulation and Control:** The government regulates healthcare providers, sets service prices, and often employs healthcare professionals.

Advantages:

1. **Equitable Access:** Public healthcare systems promote equity by ensuring that everyone, regardless of income, has access to necessary healthcare services. This reduces disparities in health outcomes.

2. **Cost Control:** The government's ability to negotiate prices and manage resources can lead to more effective cost control, reducing overall healthcare spending.

3. **Preventive Care Focus:** Public systems often emphasize preventive care and early intervention, which can improve public health outcomes and reduce long-term costs.

Challenges:

1. **Funding Constraints:** Public healthcare systems depend on government budgets, which can be limited. Economic downturns or budget cuts can affect the availability and quality of services.

2. **Bureaucracy:** Government-run systems can suffer from bureaucratic inefficiencies, leading to longer wait times and potentially lower responsiveness to patient needs.

3. **Limited Choice:** Patients in public systems may have fewer choices regarding healthcare providers and treatments compared to private systems.

Private Healthcare Systems

Characteristics:

Private healthcare systems rely on market mechanisms and private financing to provide medical services. Key features include:

1. **Market-Based Funding:** Private healthcare is funded through private insurance premiums, out-of-pocket payments, and employer-sponsored health plans.

2. **Competition:** Multiple private providers compete for patients, which can drive innovation and quality improvements.

3. **Provider Independence:** Healthcare providers operate independently, setting their own prices and service offerings.

Advantages:

1. **Choice and Flexibility:** Private healthcare systems offer patients a wide range of choices in providers, treatments, and insurance plans, allowing for personalized care.

2. **Innovation and Efficiency:** Competition among private providers can spur innovation, leading to the development of new treatments, technologies, and service delivery models.

3. **Responsiveness:** Private providers may be more responsive to patient needs and preferences, offering shorter wait times and more tailored services.

Challenges:

1. **Access and Affordability:** Private healthcare can lead to disparities in access, as those without adequate insurance or financial resources may struggle to afford necessary care.

2. **Higher Costs:** The administrative complexity and profit motives in private systems can result in higher overall healthcare costs compared to public systems.

3. **Fragmentation:** Private systems can be fragmented, with varying levels of coverage and quality, making it difficult to ensure consistent and comprehensive care for all individuals.

Hybrid Models

Many countries, including the United States, use hybrid models that incorporate elements of both public and private healthcare systems. These models aim to balance the strengths and weaknesses of each approach:

1. **Public-Private Partnerships:** Collaborations between government and private entities can enhance service delivery and innovation while ensuring broader access.

2. **Subsidized Private Insurance:** Government subsidies can help make private insurance more affordable for low- and

middle-income individuals, expanding coverage while maintaining market competition.

3. **Regulation and Oversight:** Effective regulation of private providers and insurers can help control costs, ensure quality, and protect consumers.

The choice between public and private healthcare systems involves trade-offs between equity, cost efficiency, choice, and innovation. Public systems prioritize universal access and cost control, but can face funding and bureaucratic challenges. Private systems offer greater choice and responsiveness, but can lead to disparities in access and higher costs. Hybrid models seek to combine the best aspects of both approaches, aiming to provide comprehensive, high-quality care while addressing the limitations of each system. As healthcare remains a critical issue in the 2024 US elections, understanding these differences is crucial for informed policy discussions and decision-making.

Chapter 7

Job Market and Employment Policies

The job market and employment policies are central to the economic well-being and stability of any country. They influence not only the availability of jobs and the conditions under which people work but also broader economic trends such as productivity, innovation, and income distribution. In the context of the 2024 US elections, candidates are proposing diverse strategies to address challenges in the job market, including unemployment, underemployment, wage stagnation, and the impact of automation and globalization. This chapter explores the various employment policies put forward by major candidates, examining their potential to create jobs, enhance worker protections, and promote equitable economic growth. By understanding these policies, voters can better evaluate the plans and promises of those seeking office, and consider how different approaches may affect the labour market dynamics and the broader economy in the coming years.

Strategies for Reducing Unemployment

Reducing unemployment is a critical goal for policymakers, as it directly impacts economic growth, income distribution, and social stability. Effective strategies for reducing unemployment involve a mix of short-term interventions to address immediate joblessness and long-term policies to foster a resilient and dynamic labour market. This section explores various approaches to reducing unemployment, highlighting key strategies and their potential impacts.

Short-Term Strategies

1. **Stimulus Programs:**

    - **Fiscal Stimulus:** Government spending on infrastructure projects, public services, and direct financial aid can create immediate job opportunities and boost demand in the economy. By increasing public sector employment and stimulating private sector activity, fiscal stimulus can reduce unemployment quickly.

    - **Monetary Stimulus:** Central banks can lower interest rates and engage in quantitative easing to encourage borrowing and investment. Lower borrowing costs can lead to increased business investments and consumer spending, which in turn creates jobs.

2. **Job Creation Programs:**

    - **Public Works Programs:** Governments can initiate public works projects, such as building and repairing infrastructure, to directly create jobs. These projects not only provide immediate employment but also improve long-term economic efficiency.

    - **Subsidies for Hiring:** Offering subsidies or tax incentives to businesses for hiring new employees can encourage companies to expand their workforce. Targeted subsidies can be particularly effective in promoting the employment of disadvantaged groups.

3. **Support for Small Businesses:**

    - **Access to Credit:** Ensuring that small businesses have access to affordable credit can help them grow and create jobs. Government-backed loans and grants can provide the necessary financial support for small enterprises to expand.

- **Regulatory Relief:** Simplifying regulations and reducing bureaucratic hurdles can make it easier for small businesses to operate and hire new workers. Streamlining processes for business registration, taxation, and compliance can foster a more dynamic small business sector.

Long-Term Strategies

1. **Education and Training:**

   - **Skill Development:** Investing in education and vocational training programs can equip workers with the skills needed in the modern labour market. Emphasizing STEM (science, technology, engineering, and mathematics) education and technical skills can prepare workers for high-demand jobs.

   - **Apprenticeships and Internships:** Creating partnerships between educational institutions and industries to offer apprenticeships and internships can provide practical experience and improve employability. These programs bridge the gap between education and employment, helping young people transition smoothly into the workforce.

2. **Labour Market Policies:**

   - **Unemployment Insurance:** Strengthening unemployment insurance programs can provide temporary financial support to unemployed individuals, helping them stay afloat while searching for new jobs. Well-designed unemployment benefits can also reduce the pressure to accept unsuitable jobs, leading to better job matches and long-term productivity gains.

   - **Job Placement Services:** Expanding public employment services to offer job matching, career counselling, and job search assistance can help unemployed individuals find suitable employment more quickly. These services can be particularly beneficial for long-term unemployed and disadvantaged job seekers.

3. **Economic Diversification:**

    - **Industry Development:** Promoting the development of diverse industries can reduce dependence on a single sector and create a more resilient job market. Supporting emerging industries such as technology, renewable energy, and advanced manufacturing can generate new employment opportunities.

    - **Regional Development:** Addressing regional disparities in employment by investing in economically lagging areas can create jobs and promote balanced economic growth. Regional development initiatives can include infrastructure investment, incentives for businesses to locate in underserved areas, and support for local entrepreneurship.

4. **Labour Market Flexibility:**

    - **Flexible Work Arrangements:** Encouraging flexible work arrangements, such as remote work, part-time work, and gig work, can increase labour market participation. Flexible options can help individuals balance work with other responsibilities, such as caregiving or education.

    - **Labour Mobility:** Reducing barriers to labour mobility, such as housing costs and relocation expenses, can help workers move to areas with better job opportunities. Policies that support affordable housing and relocation assistance can enhance labour market flexibility.

    Reducing unemployment requires a multifaceted approach that addresses both immediate and structural issues in the labour market. Short-term strategies like fiscal and monetary stimulus, public works programs, and support for small businesses can provide quick relief and job creation. Long-term strategies focusing on education and training, labour market policies, economic diversification, and labour market flexibility can foster a more resilient and dynamic employment landscape. By implementing a combination of these strategies, policymakers can create a robust labour market that supports sustained economic growth and broad-based prosperity. As the 2024 US elections approach, understanding these strategies is crucial for evaluating the candidates' proposals and their potential impact on unemployment.

The Gig Economy and Labour Rights

The gig economy, characterized by short-term contracts or freelance work as opposed to permanent jobs, has transformed the labour market significantly in recent years. Platforms like Uber, Lyft, and Task Rabbit have enabled millions to participate in this flexible work model. However, the rise of the gig economy has also raised important questions about labour rights and protections for gig workers. This section explores the dynamics of the gig economy, the challenges faced by gig workers, and the ongoing debates about how to ensure fair labour rights in this evolving employment landscape.

Dynamics of the Gig Economy

1. **Flexibility and Autonomy:**
   - **Work Flexibility:** Gig work offers flexibility in terms of work hours and locations, allowing individuals to balance work with other commitments such as education, caregiving, or pursuing other interests.

- **Independent Contracting:** Many gig workers value the autonomy that comes with being an independent contractor, including the ability to choose which jobs to accept and reject.

2. **Diverse Opportunities:**

   - **Variety of Jobs:** The gig economy spans various sectors, including transportation, delivery, home services, and professional freelancing. This diversity provides opportunities for people with different skills and backgrounds.

   - **Supplemental Income:** For many, gig work serves as a source of supplemental income rather than a primary job, helping to meet financial needs without committing to a full-time job.

Challenges Faced by Gig Workers

1. **Lack of Benefits:**

   - **No Access to Traditional Benefits:** Gig workers typically do not receive benefits such as health insurance, retirement plans, paid sick leave, or vacation days, which are standard for traditional employees.

   - **Financial Insecurity:** The absence of benefits and the unpredictable nature of gig work can lead to financial instability, making it challenging for workers to plan for the future or handle emergencies.

2. **Income Volatility:**

   - **Unpredictable Earnings:** Gig work often comes with income volatility, as earnings can fluctuate based on demand, platform algorithms, and competition among workers.

- **Lack of Minimum Wage Protections:** Many gig workers are not guaranteed a minimum wage, and their income may fall below the legal minimum wage in some cases after accounting for expenses.

3. **Worker Classification:**

    - **Independent Contractor Status:** Most gig workers are classified as independent contractors rather than employees. This classification limits their access to labour protections and benefits provided under employment laws.

    - **Legal and Regulatory Ambiguities:** The classification of gig workers has led to legal disputes and regulatory challenges, with different jurisdictions taking varying approaches to addressing the issue.

Debates and Policy Responses

1. **Reclassification of Workers:**

    - **Employee Status for Gig Workers:** Some policymakers and labour advocates argue that gig workers should be classified as employees to ensure they receive the same rights and protections as traditional workers. This includes access to benefits, minimum wage protections, and the right to unionize.

    - **Hybrid Models:** Proposals for hybrid models, such as creating a new category of worker that combines aspects of both employee and independent contractor status, aim to provide gig workers with some protections without fully reclassifying them as employees.

2. **Platform Accountability:**

   - **Regulating Platforms:** Governments are exploring ways to hold gig economy platforms accountable for the working conditions of their contractors. This includes enforcing transparency in payment practices, ensuring fair treatment, and providing mechanisms for dispute resolution.

   - **Portable Benefits:** Advocates suggest the creation of portable benefits systems that are tied to the worker rather than the employer. These benefits would follow the worker across different gig jobs, providing continuity and security.

3. **Collective Bargaining and Worker Voice:**

   - **Unionization Efforts:** Efforts to unionize gig workers aim to give them a collective voice to negotiate better pay, benefits, and working conditions. Examples include the formation of gig worker unions and associations.

   - **Legal Protections for Organizing:** Strengthening legal protections for gig workers to organize and bargain collectively can empower them to advocate for their rights and interests.

   The gig economy offers significant flexibility and opportunities but also presents challenges related to labour rights and protections. Addressing these challenges requires a nuanced approach that balances the benefits of gig work with the need for fair labour standards. Policymakers, platforms, and labour advocates must collaborate to develop innovative solutions that ensure gig workers have access to essential protections and benefits while preserving the flexibility that attracts many to this work model. As the 2024 US elections approach, the debate over the gig economy and labour rights will remain a critical issue, shaping the future of work and economic security for millions of Americans.

Impact of Automation on Jobs

Automation, driven by advancements in technology such as artificial intelligence (AI), robotics, and machine learning, is transforming industries and reshaping the job market. While automation offers potential for increased efficiency and economic growth, it also raises concerns about job displacement and the future of work. This section explores the multifaceted impact of automation on jobs, including job displacement, job creation, and the evolving nature of work.

Job Displacement

1. **Threat to Routine Jobs:**

    - **Repetitive Tasks:** Automation primarily affects jobs that involve routine and repetitive tasks. Occupations in manufacturing, data entry, and basic customer service are particularly vulnerable as machines and algorithms can perform these tasks more efficiently and cost-effectively.

    - **Low-Skilled Jobs:** Workers in low-skilled positions are at a higher risk of job displacement due to automation. As companies adopt automated systems, these workers may find it challenging to compete with machines that can perform the same tasks faster and without error.

2. **Sectoral Impact:**

    - **Manufacturing:** The manufacturing sector has experienced significant automation, with robots and automated systems taking over assembly line tasks. This shift has led to substantial job losses in some regions but has also created opportunities for higher-skilled positions in maintenance and oversight of automated systems.

- **Retail and Services:** In the retail sector, automated checkout systems and inventory management technologies are reducing the need for cashiers and stock clerks. Similarly, in the service industry, automated customer service agents and catboats are replacing human agents for basic inquiries.

Job Creation

1. **New Job Opportunities:**

    - **Tech and Engineering:** Automation generates demand for new jobs in technology development, implementation, and maintenance. Positions such as AI specialists, robotics engineers, and data analysts are becoming increasingly important.

    - **Advanced Manufacturing:** Automation in manufacturing has created roles that require advanced technical skills, such as programming, operating, and maintaining automated machinery. These jobs often offer higher wages and better working conditions compared to traditional manufacturing roles.

2. **Complementary Roles:**

    - **Human-Machine Collaboration:** As automation takes over routine tasks, workers can focus on more complex, creative, and interpersonal aspects of their jobs. For example, in healthcare, automation can handle administrative tasks, allowing healthcare professionals to spend more time on patient care.

    - **Service and Maintenance:** The rise of automation necessitates a workforce skilled in servicing and maintaining automated systems. These roles ensure that machines operate smoothly and efficiently, preventing downtime and increasing productivity.

Evolving Nature of Work

1. **Skills and Training:**

   - **Upskilling and Reskilling:** To adapt to the changing job market, workers need to acquire new skills and competencies. Upskilling and reskilling programs are essential for helping displaced workers transition into new roles created by automation.

   - **Lifelong Learning:** The rapid pace of technological change requires a shift towards lifelong learning. Workers must continually update their skills to remain relevant in an evolving job market.

2. **Workplace Transformation:**

   - **Remote Work:** Automation and digital technologies facilitate remote work, offering flexibility and expanding job opportunities beyond geographical boundaries. This shift can improve work-life balance and reduce commuting times.

   - **Gig Economy:** Automation contributes to the growth of the gig economy by enabling platforms that connect workers with short-term job opportunities. While this offers flexibility, it also raises concerns about job security and benefits for gig workers.

Policy Responses and Strategies

1. **Education and Training Initiatives:**

   - **Government and Industry Collaboration:** Policymakers and businesses must collaborate to develop education and training programs that prepare workers for the jobs of the future. This includes investing in STEM education, vocational training, and apprenticeship programs.

- **Public-Private Partnerships:** Partnerships between governments, educational institutions, and private companies can create training programs tailored to industry needs, ensuring a steady pipeline of skilled workers.

2. **Social Safety Nets:**

    - **Unemployment Benefits:** Strengthening unemployment benefits and social safety nets can support workers displaced by automation, providing them with financial stability while they transition to new roles.

    - **Universal Basic Income (UBI):** Some propose UBI as a solution to job displacement, offering a guaranteed income to all citizens to ensure economic security in an increasingly automated world.

    Automation significantly impacts the job market, leading to both job displacement and the creation of new opportunities. While routine and low-skilled jobs are at risk, automation also drives demand for advanced technical skills and human-machine collaboration. Adapting to these changes requires a proactive approach from policymakers, businesses, and workers, focusing on education, training, and supportive social policies. As automation continues to reshape the workforce, ensuring a smooth transition and equitable distribution of benefits will be crucial for economic stability and social well-being.

Chapter 8

Trade and Globalization

Trade and globalization have been central to economic development and international relations for decades, shaping the way countries interact, produce, and consume goods and services. As the global economy becomes increasingly interconnected, the benefits and challenges of trade and globalization are hotly debated topics, especially in the context of the 2024 US elections. Proponents argue that trade and globalization drive economic growth, create jobs, and foster innovation, while critics highlight issues such as job displacement, wage stagnation, and economic inequality. This chapter explores the complexities of trade and globalization, examining their impact on national economies, labour markets, and geopolitical dynamics. By analysing the various perspectives and policy proposals related to trade and globalization, this chapter aims to provide a comprehensive understanding of these phenomena and their implications for the future of economic policy and international cooperation. Understanding the interplay between trade and globalization is crucial for evaluating the economic platforms of the candidates and their potential impact on both domestic and global economic landscapes.

US-China Trade Relations

US-China trade relations are one of the most significant and complex economic relationships in the world. The economic interdependence between the two largest economies influences global trade patterns, economic policies, and geopolitical dynamics. This section delves into the evolution of US-China trade relations, the key issues at stake, and the potential future directions of this crucial economic partnership.

Historical Context

1. **Early Engagement:**

    - **Normalization of Relations:** The US and China normalized diplomatic relations in 1979, paving the way for increased economic engagement. China's market reforms under Deng Xiaoping further opened its economy to foreign investment and trade.

    - **China's WTO Accession:** China joined the World Trade Organization (WTO) in 2001, marking a significant milestone in US-China trade relations. This accession facilitated China's deeper integration into the global economy and increased bilateral trade.

2. **Trade Growth:**

    - **Rapid Expansion:** Over the past few decades, trade between the US and China has grown exponentially. China has become the largest trading partner of the US, with trade in goods and services amounting to hundreds of billions of dollars annually.

    - **Investment Flows:** Alongside trade, there has been substantial bilateral investment, with US companies investing in China to tap into its vast market and Chinese companies investing in the US to access technology and markets.

Key Issues in US-China Trade Relations

1. **Trade Imbalances:**

   - **US Trade Deficit:** One of the most contentious issues is the significant trade deficit the US runs with China. Critics argue that this imbalance results from unfair trade practices, while others attribute it to structural economic differences and consumption patterns.

   - **Impact on Jobs:** The trade deficit is often linked to job losses in US manufacturing sectors, fuelling debates about the benefits and drawbacks of globalization.

2. **Intellectual Property and Technology Transfer:**

   - **IP Theft:** The US has long accused China of intellectual property (IP) theft, alleging that Chinese companies have engaged in practices such as counterfeiting and forced technology transfers to gain competitive advantages.

   - **Technology Transfer Policies:** US firms operating in China have reported pressures to transfer technology as a condition for market access, leading to concerns about the loss of American technological leadership.

3. **Tariffs and Trade Barriers:**

   - **Trade War:** The US-China trade war, initiated in 2018 under the Trump administration, saw the imposition of tariffs on hundreds of billions of dollars' worth of goods. These tariffs aimed to address trade imbalances and force China to change its trade practices.

   - **Phase One Agreement:** In January 2020, the US and China signed the Phase One trade agreement, wherein China committed to purchasing more US goods and addressing some IP and technology transfer concerns. However, many underlying issues remain unresolved.

4. **Supply Chain Dependencies:**

   - **Global Supply Chains:** The COVID-19 pandemic highlighted the vulnerabilities of global supply chains, with both the US and China recognizing the need to reassess and secure their supply chains for critical goods such as medical supplies and technology components.

   - **Reshoring and Diversification:** There is a growing trend in the US to reshore manufacturing and diversify supply chains away from China to reduce dependency and enhance economic resilience.

Future Directions

1. **Strategic Competition and Cooperation:**

   - **Biden Administration's Approach:** The Biden administration has continued a tough stance on China while also seeking avenues for cooperation on global issues such as climate change and public health. The approach involves working with allies to present a united front on trade and economic policies.

   - **Technology and Innovation:** The US aims to maintain its technological edge through investment in innovation and research while addressing concerns about China's rise in high-tech industries.

2. **Trade Agreements and Multilateralism:**

   - **Reengagement with Multilateral Institutions:** The US is likely to reengage with multilateral trade institutions and agreements, promoting rules-based trade to address grievances with China.

- **Regional Partnerships:** Strengthening trade relationships with other Asian economies through initiatives like the Comprehensive and Progressive Agreement for Trans-Pacific Partnership (CPTPP) can provide alternatives to reliance on China.

US-China trade relations are characterized by deep interdependence and significant tensions. While the economic partnership has driven substantial growth and integration, it has also led to trade imbalances, IP concerns, and strategic rivalries. As the US navigates its future trade policies with China, balancing competition and cooperation will be crucial. The outcomes of these efforts will have profound implications not only for the bilateral relationship but also for global trade dynamics and economic stability.

The Future of Free Trade Agreements

Free Trade Agreements (FTAs) have been a cornerstone of global economic policy, promoting the reduction of trade barriers, the facilitation of cross-border commerce, and the fostering of economic integration. However, the future of FTAs is currently being re-evaluated amid shifting geopolitical dynamics, rising protectionism, and evolving economic priorities. This section explores the potential directions for FTAs, considering both the challenges and opportunities that lie ahead.

Shifting Geopolitical Dynamics

1. **US Trade Policy Shifts:**

    - **From Multilateral to Bilateral:** The US has historically been a proponent of multilateral FTAs, such as the North

American Free Trade Agreement (NAFTA) and its successor, the United States-Mexico-Canada Agreement (USMCA). However, recent shifts have seen a greater focus on bilateral agreements, reflecting a preference for tailored trade deals that address specific national interests.

- **Strategic Competition:** The US is likely to use FTAs as tools to counter the influence of rival powers, particularly China. This involves strengthening economic ties with allies and partners through agreements that support shared strategic objectives.

2. **European Union (EU) Trade Strategy:**

- **Sustainable Trade:** The EU is incorporating sustainability and climate goals into its trade agreements, reflecting broader commitments to environmental standards and carbon reduction. Future FTAs are expected to include stringent provisions on labour rights, environmental protection, and corporate governance.

- **Strategic Autonomy:** In response to global uncertainties, the EU aims to reduce dependencies on critical supplies from non-EU countries by diversifying its trade partnerships and strengthening intra-EU trade.

Rising Protectionism and Trade Tensions

1. **Trade Barriers and Tariffs:**

- **Protectionist Policies:** The rise of protectionist policies in various countries poses a challenge to the future of FTAs. Trade wars, such as the US-China tariff battle, have highlighted the risks of unilateral trade measures and the potential for retaliatory actions.

- **Supply Chain Security:** The COVID-19 pandemic has underscored the importance of secure and resilient supply chains. Countries are increasingly prioritizing domestic production and self-sufficiency in critical sectors, which could impact the liberalization goals of FTAs.

2. **Regional Trade Blocs:**

    - **Regional Comprehensive Economic Partnership (RCEP):** The RCEP, which includes China and other Asia-Pacific nations, represents a significant shift towards regional trade integration. As the largest FTA in terms of population and GDP, it could influence global trade patterns and challenge Western-led trade initiatives.

    - **Africa Continental Free Trade Area (AfCFTA):** The AfCFTA aims to create a single market across Africa, boosting intra-African trade and economic growth. This initiative highlights the potential for regional FTAs to drive economic development and integration in emerging markets.

Evolving Economic Priorities

1. **Digital Trade and E-Commerce:**

    - **Digital Economy:** The rise of the digital economy is reshaping trade policies. Future FTAs are likely to include comprehensive provisions on digital trade, data protection, and cybersecurity. Ensuring cross-border data flows while safeguarding privacy will be a key focus.

    - **E-Commerce Facilitation:** FTAs will increasingly address the regulatory challenges of e-commerce, aiming to harmonize standards and reduce barriers for online businesses. This includes simplifying customs procedures and promoting consumer protection in digital transactions.

2. **Sustainable and Inclusive Trade:**

    - **Environmental Standards:** Addressing climate change and promoting sustainable development are becoming central to trade agreements. Future FTAs will likely incorporate commitments to reduce carbon emissions, protect biodiversity, and promote green technologies.

    - **Social Inclusion:** Ensuring that trade benefits are broadly shared is another priority. FTAs may include stronger labour rights protections, mechanisms to support small and medium-sized enterprises (SMEs), and provisions to enhance gender and social equity.

    The future of Free Trade Agreements is being shaped by a complex interplay of geopolitical shifts, protectionist trends, and evolving economic priorities. While challenges such as rising protectionism and supply chain security concerns pose risks, opportunities exist in areas like digital trade, sustainability, and regional integration. The adaptability and responsiveness of trade policies to these changing dynamics will determine the success and relevance of FTAs in promoting global economic integration and prosperity. As nations navigate these complexities, the continued evolution of FTAs will be crucial for fostering a stable and inclusive global trade environment.

Protecting Domestic Industries

Protecting domestic industries is a crucial aspect of economic policy that seeks to safeguard a country's businesses and workforce from foreign competition. This protection can take various forms, including tariffs, subsidies, import quotas, and regulatory measures. The rationale behind these protective measures is to promote national economic security, preserve jobs, and foster the growth of key industries. However, protecting domestic industries also comes with potential drawbacks, such as higher consumer prices and retaliatory actions from trade partners. This section explores the strategies for protecting domestic industries, the benefits and challenges associated with these strategies, and their implications for economic policy.

Strategies for Protecting Domestic Industries

1. **Tariffs and Import Quotas:**

    - **Tariffs:** Imposing tariffs, or taxes on imported goods, makes foreign products more expensive compared to domestically produced goods. This price increase can help protect local industries from cheaper foreign competition.

    - **Import Quotas:** Setting limits on the quantity of specific goods that can be imported restricts foreign competition and supports domestic producers by maintaining a larger share of the market for local goods.

2. **Subsidies and Financial Support:**

    - **Direct Subsidies:** Governments can provide direct financial support to domestic industries in the form of subsidies, reducing their production costs and enhancing their competitiveness against foreign products.

    - **Tax Incentives:** Offering tax breaks or credits to domestic companies can lower their operating costs and encourage investment in local industries.

3. **Regulatory Measures:**

    - **Standards and Regulations:** Implementing stringent standards and regulations for products can make it difficult for foreign goods to enter the market, thereby protecting domestic industries. These regulations can cover safety, environmental impact, and quality standards.

- **Procurement Policies:** Governments can adopt procurement policies that prioritize purchasing from domestic suppliers, thereby supporting local industries.

4. **Anti-Dumping Measures:**

- **Anti-Dumping Duties:** When foreign companies sell products at below-market prices to gain market share (a practice known as dumping), governments can impose anti-dumping duties to protect domestic industries from unfair competition.

Benefits of Protecting Domestic Industries

1. **Job Preservation:**

- **Employment Security:** Protecting domestic industries can help preserve jobs by reducing the impact of foreign competition. This is particularly important in industries that are vital for national economic stability.

2. **Economic Diversification:**

- **Promoting Key Industries:** Protective measures can help nurture and develop key industries, such as manufacturing, technology, and agriculture, leading to a more diversified and resilient economy.

3. **National Security:**

- **Strategic Industries:** Ensuring the viability of industries critical to national security, such as defence, energy, and food production, is a key reason for protective measures. This reduces reliance on foreign suppliers for essential goods.

4. **Infant Industry Protection:**

    - **Supporting Emerging Sectors:** New or emerging industries may require protection until they become competitive in the global market. Temporary protective measures can help these "infant industries" develop and grow.

Challenges and Drawbacks

1. **Higher Consumer Prices:**

    - **Cost to Consumers:** Protective measures often lead to higher prices for goods and services, as consumers bear the cost of tariffs, quotas, and subsidies through increased prices for domestic products.

2. **Trade Retaliation:**

    - **Retaliatory Measures:** Other countries may respond to protective measures with their own tariffs and trade barriers, leading to trade wars that can hurt the global economy and reduce market access for domestic exporters.

3. **Reduced Competitiveness:**

    - **Lack of Innovation:** Prolonged protection can make domestic industries complacent, reducing their incentive to innovate and improve efficiency. This can ultimately weaken their competitiveness in the global market.

4. **Resource Allocation:**

    - **Economic Distortions:** Protective measures can distort resource allocation, directing investments to protected industries at the expense of potentially more competitive or innovative sectors.

Protecting domestic industries is a complex and multifaceted policy objective that aims to safeguard national economic interests, preserve jobs, and foster the growth of key sectors. While there are clear benefits to such protective measures, including job preservation, economic diversification, and national security, there are also significant challenges and drawbacks, such as higher consumer prices, trade retaliation, and reduced competitiveness. Policymakers must carefully balance these factors when designing and implementing protectionist policies, ensuring that they support long-term economic growth and resilience without unduly burdening consumers or stifling innovation. As global economic dynamics continue to evolve, the strategies for protecting domestic industries will remain a critical aspect of economic policy discussions and decision-making.

Chapter 9
Economic Inequality

Economic inequality, the unequal distribution of income and wealth among individuals and groups within a society, is a pressing issue that influences social stability, economic growth, and overall well-being. In recent decades, disparities in income and wealth have widened in many countries, including the United States, leading to debates about the causes, consequences, and potential solutions to this complex problem. Economic inequality affects access to education, healthcare, and opportunities, creating a cycle of disadvantage that can be difficult to break. As the 2024 US elections approach, addressing economic inequality is a central focus of policy discussions, with candidates proposing various measures to reduce disparities and promote a more equitable society. This chapter explores the dimensions of economic inequality, examining its root causes, impacts on different segments of the population, and potential policy interventions aimed at fostering greater economic equity and inclusion. Understanding economic inequality is crucial for evaluating the efficacy of proposed solutions and for creating a more just and prosperous society.

Wealth Distribution Trends

Wealth distribution trends reflect the allocation of assets and financial resources among individuals and households within an economy. These trends have significant implications for economic stability, social cohesion, and overall prosperity. Over recent decades, wealth inequality has become a prominent issue in many countries, including the United States. This section delves into the patterns of wealth distribution, factors driving these trends, and their broader economic and social impacts.

Historical Context

1. **Post-World War II Era:**

    - **Economic Boom:** Following World War II, many countries, particularly in the West, experienced significant economic growth. This period, often referred to as the "Golden Age of Capitalism," saw widespread prosperity and relatively equitable wealth distribution.

    - **Rising Middle Class:** Government policies, such as the GI Bill in the US, expanded access to education and home ownership, contributing to the growth of a robust middle class and narrowing wealth gaps.

2. **Late 20th Century:**

    - **Globalization and Technological Change:** From the 1980s onwards, globalization and technological advancements transformed economies. While these developments spurred economic growth, they also contributed to greater wealth concentration as high-skilled workers and capital owners benefited disproportionately.

    - **Policy Shifts:** Economic policies in many countries shifted towards deregulation, lower taxes on the wealthy, and reduced social safety nets. These changes often favoured capital over labour, exacerbating wealth disparities.

Recent Trends in Wealth Distribution

1. **Rising Wealth Inequality:**

    - **Top Wealth Holders:** A significant trend over the past few decades have been the increasing concentration of wealth among the top 1% and even the top 0.1% of the population. These individuals hold a disproportionate share of total wealth, driven by high earnings from capital investments, business ownership, and executive compensation.

- **Stagnation for the Middle and Lower Classes:** In contrast, wealth accumulation for the middle and lower-income households has stagnated. Factors such as wage stagnation, rising living costs, and limited access to financial assets have hindered wealth growth for these groups.

2. **Financialization of the Economy:**

    - **Asset Ownership:** The increasing importance of financial markets and investments has led to greater wealth accumulation for those with access to capital. Stocks, bonds, real estate, and other financial assets have appreciated significantly, benefiting those who own them.

    - **Debt Dynamics:** Rising household debt, particularly in the form of student loans, mortgages, and consumer credit, has also impacted wealth distribution. High debt levels can erode wealth accumulation and financial stability for many households.

3. **Demographic Factors:**

    - **Age and Wealth:** Wealth tends to accumulate with age, as older individuals have had more time to save and invest. However, younger generations, particularly Millennials and Generation Z, face unique challenges, including higher education costs and housing market barriers, which impact their wealth accumulation prospects.

    - **Racial and Gender Disparities:** Wealth distribution also varies significantly across racial and gender lines. Historical and systemic inequalities have led to substantial wealth gaps between white households and households of color, as well

Factors Driving Wealth Inequality

1. **Income Inequality:**

   - **Earnings Disparities:** Rising income inequality is a primary driver of wealth inequality. High-income individuals have greater capacity to save and invest, leading to compounded wealth growth over time.

   - **Labour Market Polarization:** Technological advancements and globalization have led to labour market polarization, where high-skill, high-wage jobs have grown, while low-skill, low-wage jobs have stagnated or declined.

2. **Tax Policies:**

   - **Regressive Taxation:** Tax policies that favour the wealthy, such as lower capital gains taxes and reduced estate taxes, have exacerbated wealth concentration. These policies allow wealthy individuals to accumulate and transfer wealth more easily.

   - **Wealth Taxation:** The absence or low rates of wealth taxes in many countries mean that accumulated wealth is not significantly taxed, allowing wealth to grow unchecked.

3. **Access to Capital and Credit:**

   - **Investment Opportunities:** Wealthy individuals have better access to investment opportunities, financial advice, and credit, which enables them to grow their wealth more effectively.

   - **Financial Exclusion:** Conversely, lower-income households often face barriers to accessing credit and financial services, limiting their ability to invest and build wealth.

Impacts of Wealth Inequality

1. **Economic Implications:**

   - **Consumption Patterns:** Wealth inequality affects consumption patterns, as wealthier individuals tend to save a larger portion of their income, while lower-income households spend a higher percentage. This can impact overall demand and economic growth.

   - **Investment and Innovation:** High levels of wealth concentration can lead to investment in speculative financial assets rather than productive investments in innovation and business expansion, potentially stifling economic dynamism.

2. **Social and Political Implications:**

   - **Social Mobility:** Wealth inequality can hinder social mobility, making it difficult for individuals from lower-income backgrounds to improve their economic status. This perpetuates intergenerational poverty and inequality.

   - **Political Influence:** Concentrated wealth can lead to disproportionate political influence for the wealthy, affecting policy decisions and reinforcing economic inequalities.

Potential Policy Interventions

1. **Progressive Taxation:**

   - **Income and Wealth Taxes:** Implementing more progressive income taxes and introducing or increasing taxes on wealth, such as capital gains, estate taxes, and wealth taxes, can help reduce wealth concentration.

- **Tax Credits and Deductions:** Expanding tax credits and deductions for low- and middle-income households can help improve their financial stability and capacity for wealth accumulation.

2. **Education and Training:**

    - **Access to Quality Education:** Investing in quality education and training programs, particularly for disadvantaged communities, can improve economic opportunities and enable greater wealth accumulation.

    - **Lifelong Learning:** Supporting lifelong learning and skills development can help individuals adapt to changing labour market demands and improve their earning potential.

3. **Financial Inclusion:**

    - **Access to Credit:** Expanding access to affordable credit and financial services for low-income households can facilitate investment in education, housing, and entrepreneurship.

    - **Financial Literacy:** Promoting financial literacy can help individuals make informed decisions about saving, investing, and managing debt.

4. **Social Safety Nets:**

    - **Social Insurance Programs:** Strengthening social insurance programs, such as unemployment insurance, health insurance, and retirement benefits, can provide financial security and reduce wealth disparities.

    - **Universal Basic Income (UBI):** Proposals for UBI aim to provide a guaranteed income to all citizens, helping to ensure a basic standard of living and reducing economic inequality.

Wealth distribution trends reveal significant and growing disparities in many countries, driven by factors such as income inequality, tax policies, and access to capital. These trends have far-reaching economic, social, and political implications, impacting consumption patterns, social mobility, and political influence. Addressing wealth inequality requires a comprehensive approach, including progressive taxation, investment in education and training, financial inclusion initiatives, and robust social safety nets. As wealth inequality remains a critical issue in contemporary economic policy debates, understanding these trends and their underlying drivers is essential for crafting effective solutions to promote a more equitable and prosperous society.

Policies to Address Poverty

Addressing poverty is a complex and multifaceted challenge that requires comprehensive and sustained efforts across various policy areas. Effective anti-poverty policies must address the root causes of poverty, provide immediate relief to those in need, and create pathways for economic mobility. This section explores a range of policies aimed at reducing poverty, examining their mechanisms, impacts, and potential for fostering long-term economic stability and social equity.

Income Support and Social Safety Nets

1. **Universal Basic Income (UBI):**

    - **Definition:** UBI involves providing all citizens with a regular, unconditional cash payment, regardless of their income or employment status. This ensures a basic level of economic security for everyone.

    - **Benefits:** UBI can reduce poverty by providing a stable source of income, helping individuals meet their basic needs and reducing financial stress. It can also support economic activity by increasing consumer spending.

- **Challenges:** Implementing UBI requires substantial funding, which may necessitate significant changes to tax systems or reallocation of government spending. Additionally, there are debates about the potential disincentive effects on work.

2. **Earned Income Tax Credit (EITC):**

    - **Definition:** The EITC is a refundable tax credit for low- to moderate-income working individuals and families, designed to encourage and reward work.

    - **Benefits:** The EITC has been shown to lift millions of people out of poverty by supplementing low wages, thereby increasing disposable income for working families. It also incentivizes employment and can reduce reliance on other welfare programs.

    - **Challenges:** While effective, the EITC requires eligible individuals to file tax returns, which can be a barrier for some. Expanding outreach and simplifying the application process are critical for maximizing its impact.

3. **Social Security and Disability Benefits:**

    - **Definition:** Social Security provides retirement, disability, and survivors benefits, acting as a critical safety net for older adults and individuals with disabilities.

    - **Benefits:** Social Security is a key anti-poverty tool, particularly for seniors. It ensures a basic income for those who can no longer work, reducing poverty rates among the elderly and disabled.

- **Challenges:** Ensuring the long-term sustainability of Social Security requires addressing funding shortfalls, potentially through adjustments to payroll taxes or benefit structures.

Employment and Wage Policies

1. **Minimum Wage Increases:**

    - **Definition:** Raising the minimum wage sets a higher floor for earnings, ensuring that all workers receive a wage that meets basic living standards.

    - **Benefits:** Increasing the minimum wage can reduce poverty by boosting incomes for the lowest-paid workers, enhancing their ability to afford essentials such as housing, food, and healthcare.

    - **Challenges:** Critics argue that higher minimum wages could lead to job losses or reduced hours as businesses adjust to increased labour costs. Policymakers must balance wage increases with measures to support small businesses and mitigate potential negative impacts on employment.

2. **Job Training and Workforce Development:**

    - **Definition:** These programs provide education and training to help individuals acquire skills needed for higher-paying jobs and career advancement.

    - **Benefits:** By equipping workers with in-demand skills, job training programs can enhance employability, increase earning potential, and reduce dependency on welfare programs.

    - **Challenges:** Effective job training requires alignment with labour market demands and accessible, high-quality training options. Ongoing evaluation and adaptation of programs are essential to ensure they meet the needs of both workers and employers.

Education Policies

1. **Universal Pre-K and Early Childhood Education:**

    - **Definition:** Providing access to high-quality early childhood education for all children, regardless of family income.

    - **Benefits:** Early education is crucial for cognitive and social development, setting the foundation for future academic success and reducing achievement gaps. It also supports working parents by providing reliable childcare.

    - **Challenges:** Expanding access to universal pre-K requires significant investment in facilities, training for educators, and development of curricula. Ensuring equitable access and quality across different regions and demographics is also critical.

2. **Affordable Higher Education:**

    - **Definition:** Policies aimed at reducing the cost of higher education, such as tuition-free community college, expanded scholarships, and student loan forgiveness.

    - **Benefits:** Making higher education more affordable can increase access, particularly for low-income students, leading to better employment opportunities and higher lifetime earnings.

    - **Challenges:** Funding these initiatives requires careful budgeting and potential reallocations of public funds. Ensuring that quality education is maintained while expanding access is also essential.

Housing Policies

1. **Affordable Housing Initiatives:**

    - **Definition:** Programs that increase the supply of affordable housing through subsidies, tax credits, and public-private partnerships.

    - **Benefits:** Affordable housing reduces the financial burden on low-income households, allowing them to allocate more resources to other essentials and improving overall quality of life.

    - **Challenges:** Addressing housing affordability requires significant investment and coordination between federal, state, and local governments. Overcoming zoning restrictions and community opposition can also be challenging.

2. **Housing Vouchers and Rental Assistance:**

    - **Definition:** Programs that provide financial assistance to help low-income families afford private rental housing.

    - **Benefits:** Housing vouchers can offer immediate relief to families struggling with housing costs, promoting stability and reducing homelessness.

    - **Challenges:** Ensuring adequate funding and expanding program reach are key challenges. Additionally, finding landlords willing to accept vouchers can be difficult in some areas.

Healthcare Policies

1. **Medicaid Expansion:**

    - **Definition:** Expanding Medicaid eligibility to cover more low-income individuals and families, as allowed under the Affordable Care Act (ACA).

    - **Benefits:** Medicaid expansion improves access to healthcare, reducing medical expenses and financial strain for low-income households. It also contributes to better health outcomes, which can enhance productivity and economic stability.

    - **Challenges:** Expanding Medicaid requires state-level cooperation and funding. Political resistance and budget constraints can hinder efforts to broaden coverage.

2. **Universal Healthcare:**

    - **Definition:** Implementing a system that provides comprehensive healthcare coverage to all citizens, regardless of income or employment status.

    - **Benefits:** Universal healthcare ensures that everyone has access to necessary medical services, reducing financial barriers to care and promoting overall public health.

    - **Challenges:** Establishing universal healthcare involves substantial funding, which may require new taxes or reallocations of existing resources. Balancing cost control with quality and accessibility is also a major consideration.

Social and Economic Inclusion Policies

1. **Anti-Discrimination and Equal Opportunity:**

    - **Definition:** Policies that promote equal opportunity in education, employment, and housing, and protect individuals from discrimination based on race, gender, disability, and other factors.

    - **Benefits:** Ensuring equal access to opportunities helps reduce systemic barriers to economic mobility and promotes a more inclusive society.

    - **Challenges:** Effective enforcement of anti-discrimination laws and addressing implicit biases require ongoing effort and commitment from both public and private sectors.

2. **Support for Marginalized Communities:**

    - **Definition:** Targeted programs that address the specific needs of marginalized groups, such as Indigenous populations, and people of colour.

    - **Benefits:** Tailored support can help address unique challenges faced by marginalized communities, promoting equity and reducing disparities in income, health, and education.

    - **Challenges:** Ensuring that programs are culturally sensitive and effectively reach target populations requires collaboration with community organizations and continuous evaluation.

        Addressing poverty requires a multifaceted approach that combines immediate relief with long-term strategies for economic mobility and inclusion. Income support and social safety nets, employment and wage policies, education initiatives, housing programs, healthcare reforms, and social and economic inclusion policies all play critical roles in reducing poverty and promoting equity. By implementing comprehensive and coordinated policies, governments can create a more just and prosperous society where all individuals have the opportunity to thrive. As the 2024 US elections approach, the effectiveness and feasibility of these policies will be central to the debate on how to address poverty and economic inequality in America.

The Impact of Education on Economic Mobility

Education is widely regarded as a fundamental driver of economic mobility, offering individuals the skills, knowledge, and credentials needed to improve their economic standing and achieve upward mobility. The relationship between education and economic mobility is multifaceted, encompassing various stages of the education system, from early childhood education to higher education and beyond. This section explores how education impacts economic mobility, the mechanisms through which it operates, and the challenges and policy interventions that can enhance its effectiveness.

Early Childhood Education

1. **Foundation for Future Learning:**

    - **Cognitive and Social Development:** Early childhood education (ECE) provides critical cognitive and social development opportunities that set the foundation for future academic success. High-quality ECE programs help children develop essential skills such as language, numeracy, and social interaction.
    - **Long-Term Benefits:** Research indicates that children who attend high-quality preschool programs are more likely to perform better academically, graduate from high school, and

pursue higher education. These long-term benefits translate into better employment opportunities and higher earnings.

2. **Reducing Achievement Gaps:**

   - **Equitable Access:** Access to quality early childhood education can reduce achievement gaps between children from different socioeconomic backgrounds. By providing all children with a strong start, ECE helps level the playing field and promotes greater equality of opportunity.

   - **Parental Support:** ECE programs often include parental engagement components, which support parents in fostering a positive home learning environment. This holistic approach enhances the overall impact of early education on children's development.

K-12 Education

1. **Academic Achievement:**

   - **Quality of Schools:** The quality of K-12 education significantly influences academic achievement and future economic outcomes. Well-resourced schools with effective teachers, rigorous curricula, and supportive environments help students develop critical thinking skills and a strong academic foundation.

   - **Standardized Testing and Accountability:** Systems of standardized testing and accountability aim to ensure that all students achieve a certain level of proficiency in core subjects. While these measures can drive improvements, they also need to be balanced with a broader focus on holistic education.

2. **High School Graduation:**

   - **Importance of Completion:** High school graduation is a critical milestone for economic mobility. Graduating from high school significantly increases the likelihood of securing stable employment and accessing higher education opportunities.

   - **Dropout Prevention:** Programs aimed at reducing dropout rates, such as mentorship, tutoring, and alternative education pathways, are essential for keeping at-risk students engaged and on track to graduate.

3. **Career and Technical Education (CTE):**

   - **Vocational Training:** CTE programs provide students with practical skills and training in specific trades or professions. These programs can offer pathways to well-paying jobs that do not necessarily require a four-year college degree.

   - **Work-Based Learning:** Partnerships between schools and industries that offer apprenticeships and internships can enhance CTE programs, providing students with real-world experience and connections to potential employers.

Higher Education

1. **Access to Postsecondary Education:**

   - **College Enrollment and Completion:** Access to higher education is a key determinant of economic mobility. Individuals with a college degree typically earn significantly higher wages than those with only a high school diploma. However, barriers such as high tuition costs and inadequate preparation can hinder college enrollment and completion.

- **Financial Aid and Scholarships:** Financial aid programs, including grants, scholarships, and student loans, are crucial for making higher education accessible to low- and middle-income students. Ensuring that these programs are adequately funded and effectively administered is essential for promoting equity in higher education access.

2. **Quality of Education:**

    - **Institutional Quality:** The quality of higher education institutions, including faculty expertise, research opportunities, and student support services, impacts the value of the education received. Attending high-quality institutions can enhance students' learning experiences and employment prospects.

    - **Field of Study:** The field of study also influences economic outcomes. Degrees in STEM (science, technology, engineering, and mathematics), business, and healthcare tend to offer higher earning potential compared to fields such as the humanities and social sciences.

3. **Graduate Education and Lifelong Learning:**

    - **Advanced Degrees:** Pursuing graduate education can further enhance economic mobility by opening up opportunities for specialized, high-paying careers. Fields such as law, medicine, and engineering often require advanced degrees for entry.

    - **Continuing Education:** Lifelong learning and continuing education programs help individuals adapt to changing labour market demands and advance their careers. These programs are especially important in industries experiencing rapid technological change.

Challenges to Economic Mobility through Education

1. **Educational Inequities:**

    - **Resource Disparities:** Significant disparities in funding and resources between schools in affluent areas and those in low-income communities contribute to unequal educational outcomes. Addressing these disparities is critical for ensuring that all students have access to high-quality education.

    - **Segregation and Inequality:** Racial and socioeconomic segregation in schools perpetuates educational inequalities. Policies aimed at promoting school integration and equitable resource allocation are necessary to tackle these issues.

2. **Affordability of Higher Education:**

    - **Rising Tuition Costs:** The increasing cost of higher education is a major barrier to college access and completion. High levels of student debt can also limit economic mobility by reducing graduates' financial flexibility.

    - **Financial Literacy:** Improving financial literacy among students and families can help them make informed decisions about college financing and manage debt effectively.

3. **Systemic Barriers:**

    - **Discrimination and Bias:** Systemic discrimination and bias in educational institutions and the labour market can hinder the economic mobility of marginalized groups. Efforts to promote diversity, equity, and inclusion are essential for creating a fairer education system and society.

- **Support Systems:** Providing comprehensive support systems, including academic advising, mental health services, and career counselling, is crucial for helping students overcome barriers and succeed in their educational and career pursuits.

Policy Interventions to Enhance Economic Mobility through Education

1. **Early Childhood Education Investments:**

   - **Universal Pre-K:** Expanding access to universal pre-K programs can ensure that all children receive high-quality early education, laying a strong foundation for future success.

   - **Parent Engagement Programs:** Supporting parent engagement initiatives can enhance the effectiveness of early childhood education by involving families in their children's learning and development.

2. **K-12 Education Reforms:**

   - **Equitable Funding:** Implementing policies that ensure equitable funding for all schools, regardless of local property tax revenues, can reduce resource disparities and improve educational outcomes.

   - **Teacher Training and Support:** Investing in teacher training and professional development can enhance instructional quality and student achievement.

3. **Higher Education Access and Affordability:**

   - **Tuition-Free Community College:** Offering tuition-free community college can expand access to higher education and provide a pathway to four-year degrees and well-paying jobs.

- **Expanded Financial Aid:** Increasing funding for need-based financial aid programs and simplifying the application process can make higher education more accessible to low- and middle-income students.

4. **Workforce Development and Adult Education:**

    - **Skills Training Programs:** Supporting skills training and vocational education programs can help workers acquire in-demand skills and improve their employment prospects.

    - **Continuing Education and Lifelong Learning:** Promoting continuing education and lifelong learning initiatives can help individuals adapt to changing job markets and advance their careers.

    Education is a powerful driver of economic mobility, offering individuals the opportunity to improve their economic standing and achieve upward mobility. From early childhood education to higher education and beyond, various stages of the education system play crucial roles in shaping economic outcomes. However, significant challenges, including educational inequities, affordability barriers, and systemic discrimination, must be addressed to fully realize the potential of education as a tool for economic mobility. Policymakers must implement comprehensive and equitable education policies to ensure that all individuals have the opportunity to succeed and thrive in an ever-changing economy. As society continues to evolve, investing in education will remain essential for fostering a more equitable and prosperous future.

Chapter 10
Environmental Economics

Environmental economics is a field of study that examines the economic impacts of environmental policies and the ways economic activities affect the environment. This discipline seeks to balance economic growth with environmental sustainability, addressing issues such as pollution, natural resource management, and climate change. By applying economic principles to environmental challenges, policymakers can design effective strategies that promote both economic prosperity and ecological health. The 2024 US elections bring renewed focus on environmental economics, with candidates proposing various policies to tackle climate change, protect natural resources, and transition to a sustainable economy. This chapter explores the key concepts and debates in environmental economics, including the valuation of ecosystem services, the role of market-based instruments like carbon pricing, and the economic implications of transitioning to renewable energy sources. Understanding these dynamics is crucial for developing policies that support a sustainable future while fostering economic resilience and growth.

The Economics of Climate Change Mitigation

Climate change mitigation refers to efforts to reduce or prevent the emission of greenhouse gases (GHGs) to curb global warming. As climate change poses significant risks to economies, ecosystems, and communities worldwide, addressing it requires comprehensive economic strategies that balance environmental protection with economic growth. This section delves into the economics of climate change mitigation, exploring the costs, benefits, and policy instruments involved, as well as the implications for various sectors and stakeholders.

Costs of Climate Change Mitigation

1. **Initial Investment:**

    - **Infrastructure and Technology:** Transitioning to low-carbon technologies and infrastructure requires substantial upfront investment. This includes renewable energy installations (e.g., solar panels, wind turbines), energy-efficient buildings, and electric vehicle (EV) charging networks.

    - **Research and Development:** Innovation in clean technologies and sustainable practices demands significant funding for research and development. These investments are crucial for advancing technologies that can reduce emissions more effectively and economically.

2. **Economic Adjustment:**

    - **Industry Adaptation:** Industries reliant on fossil fuels, such as coal mining and oil production, face significant transition costs. These sectors must invest in new technologies or diversify their activities to align with low-carbon goals.

    - **Job Displacement:** Shifting to a low-carbon economy may lead to job losses in traditional energy sectors. While new jobs will be created in renewable energy and other green industries, there is a need for retraining and support for displaced workers.

3. **Policy Implementation:**

    - **Regulatory Costs:** Implementing and enforcing new regulations, such as emission standards and carbon pricing mechanisms, incurs administrative costs for governments and compliance costs for businesses.

    - **Subsidies and Incentives:** Governments may need to provide financial incentives, such as subsidies for renewable energy and tax credits for energy-efficient practices, to encourage the adoption of low-carbon technologies.

Benefits of Climate Change Mitigation

1. **Long-Term Economic Gains:**

    - **Avoided Costs of Climate Impacts:** Mitigating climate change can prevent severe economic damages associated with extreme weather events, sea-level rise, and disruptions to agriculture and water supply. These avoided costs can far outweigh the initial mitigation investments.

    - **Health Benefits:** Reducing air pollution from fossil fuel combustion leads to significant health benefits, including lower rates of respiratory and cardiovascular diseases. This can reduce healthcare costs and increase labour productivity.

2. **Economic Opportunities:**

    - **Green Jobs:** The transition to a low-carbon economy creates numerous job opportunities in renewable energy, energy efficiency, and sustainable agriculture. These "green jobs" can drive economic growth and provide stable employment.

    - **Innovation and Competitiveness:** Investing in clean technologies fosters innovation and positions countries and companies at the forefront of emerging markets. This can enhance competitiveness and open new export opportunities.

3. **Energy Security:**

   - **Reduced Dependency on Fossil Fuels:** Shifting to renewable energy sources reduces dependency on imported fossil fuels, enhancing energy security and reducing exposure to volatile global energy prices.

   - **Diversification of Energy Supply:** A diversified energy mix, including solar, wind, hydro, and geothermal, increases resilience against supply disruptions and price fluctuations.

Policy Instruments for Climate Change Mitigation

1. **Carbon Pricing:**

   - **Carbon Tax:** A carbon tax directly sets a price on carbon by taxing GHG emissions. This provides a financial incentive for businesses and individuals to reduce emissions and invest in cleaner technologies.

   - **Cap-and-Trade:** Cap-and-trade systems set a limit (cap) on total emissions and allow companies to buy and sell emission permits. This market-based approach creates economic incentives for emission reductions and encourages cost-effective mitigation strategies.

2. **Regulatory Measures:**

   - **Emission Standards:** Governments can impose regulations that set limits on emissions from industries, power plants, and vehicles. These standards can drive technological innovation and reduce pollution.

   - **Renewable Energy Mandates:** Mandating a certain percentage of energy to come from renewable sources can

accelerate the transition to clean energy. Renewable Portfolio Standards (RPS) are a common policy tool in this regard.

3. **Subsidies and Incentives:**

    - **Renewable Energy Subsidies:** Financial support for renewable energy projects, such as grants, loans, and tax credits, can reduce the cost barrier for adopting clean technologies.

    - **Energy Efficiency Programs:** Incentives for energy-efficient appliances, building retrofits, and industrial processes can significantly reduce energy consumption and emissions.

4. **Investment in Research and Development:**

    - **Public Funding for Innovation:** Government funding for research and development in clean technologies is essential for advancing new solutions that can reduce emissions more effectively and economically.

    - **Public-Private Partnerships:** Collaborations between governments, research institutions, and the private sector can leverage resources and expertise to accelerate innovation and deployment of low-carbon technologies.

Sectoral Implications

1. **Energy Sector:**

    - **Renewable Energy Transition:** The energy sector is central to climate change mitigation efforts. Transitioning from fossil fuels to renewable energy sources like solar, wind, and hydro is crucial for reducing emissions.

    - **Grid Modernization:** Upgrading the electricity grid to accommodate decentralized and intermittent renewable energy sources is essential for ensuring reliability and efficiency.

2. **Transportation:**

    - **Electrification of Vehicles:** Promoting electric vehicles (EVs) and investing in charging infrastructure can significantly reduce emissions from the transportation sector.

    - **Public Transit and Mobility:** Expanding public transit systems and promoting sustainable mobility options, such as cycling and walking, can reduce reliance on private vehicles and lower emissions.

3. **Agriculture and Forestry:**

    - **Sustainable Farming Practices:** Implementing practices like conservation tillage, crop rotation, and precision agriculture can reduce emissions from agriculture while enhancing productivity.

    - **Reforestation and Afforestation:** Planting trees and restoring forests can sequester carbon dioxide, contributing to climate change mitigation and providing additional environmental benefits.

4. **Industry:**

    - **Decarbonizing Industrial Processes:** Adopting cleaner production technologies, improving energy efficiency, and utilizing low-carbon materials can reduce emissions from industrial activities.

    - **Circular Economy:** Promoting the circular economy, which emphasizes recycling, reuse, and reducing waste, can decrease resource consumption and emissions.

Challenges and Considerations

1. **Economic and Social Equity:**

   - **Just Transition:** Ensuring a just transition for workers and communities affected by the shift from fossil fuels to clean energy is crucial. Policies should include retraining programs, social protection measures, and support for economic diversification.

   - **Global Cooperation:** Climate change is a global challenge that requires coordinated international efforts. Developed countries must support developing nations in their mitigation efforts through technology transfer, financial assistance, and capacity-building initiatives.

2. **Political Will and Public Support:**

   - **Policy Stability:** Long-term success in climate change mitigation depends on consistent and stable policies. Frequent changes in policy direction can undermine investment and progress.

   - **Public Awareness and Engagement:** Educating the public about the benefits of climate change mitigation and fostering community engagement are essential for building broad-based support for necessary measures.

Renewable Energy Investments

Investing in renewable energy is crucial for transitioning to a sustainable and low-carbon future. Renewable energy sources, such as solar, wind, hydro, and geothermal, offer numerous environmental and economic benefits, including reducing greenhouse gas emissions, enhancing energy security, and creating jobs. This section explores the key aspects of renewable energy investments, including the drivers, challenges, and potential impacts on the economy and the environment.

Drivers of Renewable Energy Investments

1. **Environmental Benefits:**

   - **Reducing Emissions:** Renewable energy sources generate electricity without emitting greenhouse gases, significantly reducing the carbon footprint of the energy sector. This is essential for mitigating climate change and meeting international climate targets, such as those outlined in the Paris Agreement.

   - **Pollution Reduction:** Renewables also help reduce air and water pollution, improving public health and reducing healthcare costs associated with respiratory and cardiovascular diseases.

2. **Economic Benefits:**

   - **Job Creation:** The renewable energy sector is a significant source of job creation. According to the International Renewable Energy Agency (IRENA), renewable energy jobs worldwide have been increasing steadily, offering opportunities in manufacturing, installation, maintenance, and research.

   - **Energy Security:** Investing in renewables reduces reliance on imported fossil fuels, enhancing national energy security and reducing exposure to volatile global energy markets.

3. **Technological Advancements:**

   - **Cost Reductions:** Technological advancements have significantly reduced the costs of renewable energy technologies, making them more competitive with traditional fossil fuels. For example, the cost of solar photovoltaic (PV) panels and wind turbines has decreased dramatically over the past decade.

- **Efficiency Improvements:** Continued research and development (R&D) are improving the efficiency of renewable energy systems, increasing their capacity to generate electricity from the same amount of resources.

Challenges of Renewable Energy Investments

1. **Intermittency and Reliability:**

    - **Variable Output:** The output of renewable energy sources like solar and wind is variable and dependent on weather conditions. This intermittency can pose challenges for grid stability and reliability.

    - **Energy Storage:** To address intermittency, investments in energy storage technologies, such as batteries and pumped hydro storage, are critical. These technologies can store excess energy generated during peak production times and release it when needed.

2. **Initial Capital Costs:**

    - **High Upfront Investment:** Despite decreasing costs, renewable energy projects still require significant upfront capital investment. This can be a barrier for deployment, especially in developing countries or regions with limited access to financing.

    - **Financing Solutions:** Innovative financing solutions, such as green bonds, public-private partnerships, and international climate finance, can help overcome this barrier by providing the necessary funding for renewable energy projects.

3. **Grid Integration:**

   - **Infrastructure Upgrades:** Integrating large amounts of renewable energy into existing power grids requires significant upgrades to grid infrastructure. This includes enhancing grid flexibility, developing smart grid technologies, and expanding transmission networks to connect renewable energy projects to demand centers.

   - **Policy and Regulation:** Supportive policies and regulatory frameworks are essential for facilitating the integration of renewables into the grid. This includes policies that promote grid modernization and provide incentives for renewable energy development.

Economic and Environmental Impacts

1. **Economic Growth:**

   - **Local Economies:** Renewable energy investments can stimulate local economies by creating jobs, attracting investments, and generating tax revenues. Rural areas, in particular, can benefit from renewable energy projects that provide new economic opportunities and infrastructure development.

   - **Diversification:** Diversifying the energy mix with renewable sources reduces economic risks associated with dependency on fossil fuels and enhances the resilience of the energy sector.

2. **Environmental Sustainability:**

   - **Biodiversity and Land Use:** Renewable energy projects, especially large-scale installations, must consider their impact on land use and biodiversity. Proper site selection and environmental impact assessments are crucial for minimizing negative effects on ecosystems.

- **Water Resources:** Renewables like solar and wind have minimal water usage compared to conventional power plants, making them more sustainable in regions facing water scarcity.

Balancing Economic Growth with Environmental Protection

Balancing economic growth with environmental protection is a complex yet essential task for sustainable development. As economies expand, the demand for resources and energy increases, often leading to environmental degradation. However, it is possible to achieve economic growth while minimizing environmental impacts through sustainable practices, policies, and technological innovations. This section explores strategies for harmonizing economic development with environmental stewardship.

Sustainable Development Framework

1. Decoupling Growth from Resource Use:

- **Resource Efficiency:** Enhancing resource efficiency involves using materials and energy more effectively to produce goods and services. This can be achieved through technological advancements, improved manufacturing processes, and better management practices.

- **Circular Economy:** Transitioning to a circular economy model, where waste is minimized and materials are reused and recycled, can significantly reduce the environmental footprint of economic activities. This approach not only conserves resources but also creates new economic opportunities in recycling and remanufacturing industries.

2. **Integrating Environmental Costs:**

    - **Internalizing Externalities:** Environmental costs, such as pollution and resource depletion, are often externalized, meaning they are not reflected in the prices of goods and services. Policies that internalize these costs, such as carbon pricing and pollution taxes, incentivize businesses to reduce their environmental impact.

    - **Eco-labeling and Green Certification:** Implementing eco-labeling and green certification programs can help consumers make informed choices about the environmental impact of their purchases. This, in turn, encourages companies to adopt sustainable practices to meet consumer demand.

Policy and Regulatory Approaches

1. **Environmental Regulations:**

    - **Emission Standards:** Setting strict emission standards for industries can drive the adoption of cleaner technologies and reduce pollution. Regulatory frameworks need to be robust and enforced effectively to ensure compliance.

    - **Protected Areas and Biodiversity Conservation:** Establishing protected areas and enforcing biodiversity conservation laws help preserve ecosystems and wildlife. These areas also offer economic benefits through eco-tourism and sustainable resource use.

2. **Incentives for Green Investments:**

    - **Subsidies and Tax Incentives:** Governments can promote green investments by offering subsidies and tax incentives for renewable energy projects, energy-efficient technologies, and sustainable agriculture practices.

- **Public-Private Partnerships:** Collaborations between the public and private sectors can leverage resources and expertise to develop and implement sustainable projects. These partnerships can drive innovation and scale up sustainable solutions.

Technological Innovations

1. **Clean Energy Technologies:**

   - **Renewable Energy:** Investing in renewable energy sources such as solar, wind, and hydro can significantly reduce greenhouse gas emissions and reliance on fossil fuels. These technologies are becoming increasingly cost-competitive and scalable.

   - **Energy Storage:** Advances in energy storage technologies, such as batteries, are crucial for integrating renewable energy into the grid and ensuring a stable energy supply.

2. **Sustainable Agriculture and Industry:**

   - **Precision Agriculture:** Utilizing precision agriculture techniques, which involve data-driven farming practices, can enhance crop yields while reducing the use of water, fertilizers, and pesticides.

   - **Green Manufacturing:** Adopting green manufacturing practices, such as using environmentally friendly materials and processes, can reduce industrial pollution and resource consumption.

Socio-Economic Considerations

1. **Inclusive Growth:**

   - **Green Jobs:** The transition to a green economy creates new job opportunities in renewable energy, energy efficiency, and sustainable agriculture. Policies should support workforce development and retraining programs to help workers transition to these emerging sectors.

- **Equitable Access to Resources:** Ensuring equitable access to clean water, air, and energy is essential for social stability and economic development. Policies should address disparities and provide support to vulnerable communities.

2. **Community Engagement:**

    - **Public Participation:** Engaging communities in environmental decision-making processes fosters a sense of ownership and responsibility. Public participation can lead to more effective and locally appropriate solutions.

    - **Education and Awareness:** Raising awareness about environmental issues and promoting sustainability education can empower individuals to make environmentally conscious decisions in their daily lives.

www.ingramcontent.com/pod-product-compliance
Lightning Source LLC
LaVergne TN
LVHW061528070526
838199LV00009B/419